THE AMERICAN ATTITUDE

The Story of the Making of
Foreign Policy in the United States

Benjamin Franklin

The

The Story of the Making of
Foreign Policy in the United States
☆ ☆ ☆ *with photographs* ☆ ☆ ☆

Edwin P. Hoyt

ABELARD-SCHUMAN
London   New York   Toronto

Other books by Edwin P. Hoyt

John Tyler
Leland Stanford
The Tragic Commodore,
The Story of Oliver Hazard Perry
American Steamboat Stories

© Copyright 1970 by Edwin P. Hoyt
Library of Congress Catalogue Card Number: 70-123516
ISBN   0 200 71694 8

The author and publisher wish to thank the United States Department
of State for the photographs, with the exception of the frontispiece,
which appear in this book.

LONDON	NEW YORK	TORONTO
Abelard-Schuman	Abelard-Schuman	Abelard-Schuman
Limited	Limited	Canada Limited
8 King St. WC2	257 Park Ave. So.	228 Yorkland Blvd.

An Intext Publisher

Printed in the United States of America

Contents

Preface

The purpose of this book is to show how the various foreign policies of the United States of America developed, and the influence exerted on the making of these policies by the men who have held the office of Secretary of State.

Under the American system the President of the United States is the Chief Executive, and that means that the President is responsible, in the final analysis, for American foreign policy. Yet it is obvious in the twentieth century that the President, though he is one of the most powerful men in the world, still depends on advisers, and that is where the influence of the Secretary of State comes in. Under some administrations, as will be seen, the Secretary of State actually made the policies and carried them out. Under other administrations, the Secretary of State was little more than the servant of the President, doing as he was told, with the President making his own policies. And in some cases, Presidents found it to their liking to circumvent the Department of State altogether in the making of foreign policy.

The complexities and changes in modern times are so great that it is impossible to discuss in any depth the making of all the policies in the twentieth century, and the series of events that shaped United States foreign policies in the 1950's and 1960's. The very term "foreign policy" indicates that the United States had a policy of some sort toward every nation —be it even one of ignoring a nation. It is much easier to deal with minute incidents of the nineteenth century than it is to evaluate twentieth-century policies, because the effects of those twentieth-century policies are still very much at hand —and so only a brief overview of events since World War II can be included.

There are no secrets to be unveiled in this book, but a reader may find some interesting additions to his store of knowledge about the way in which national policies have been made, the accidents and decisions that sometimes go into making them, the clashes of personality which have brought about crises and changes in direction, and the all-important matter of character. For when it has come to the line, foreign policy has largely been a matter of character, the character of the President, the character of the Secretary of State, and, most important of all in the long run, the character of the American people.

The development of foreign policies that can be called particularly *American* began before the establishment of the republic, and by far the most important figure in the early development of American policies was Benjamin Franklin, who is not often considered in this role. Many men followed Franklin, some able, some not so able. Both kinds left their marks on American policy making, and those marks may be seen even to this day, as these pages will reveal.

Older Than the Republic

In the spring of 1756, the assembly of the colony of Pennsylvania was deeply involved in a dispute with Governor William Shirley, who represented the crown and the Penn family, the absentee landlords who lived in England. The dispute involved high expenses for defense of the colony, and heavy taxation of the colonists by the English Parliament, where the colonists were not represented.

One of the loudest and most effective complainers was Benjamin Franklin. He was an editor, a scientist, a businessman, and a member of the Pennsylvania assembly, the legislative body. He was a sharp critic of the Penn family, and the heirs of William Penn feared and hated him.

In December, 1756, the governor of Pennsylvania asked the assembly to raise £125,000 for the coming year. The assemblymen said they could not afford so much and voted instead only £100,000. The governor vetoed the bill in January, 1757, as providing too little money and said he was sending a copy of the bill to the king to show him how disloyal the colonists had become.

9

The assembly then voted to send commissioners to London to argue their case. They named Isaac Norris, Speaker of the Assembly, and Benjamin Franklin. Norris declined because of age and health. Franklin said he would go.

On April 4, 1757, Benjamin Franklin and his son William took the coach to New York, where they then took a packet boat to England. Franklin was 51 years old. He was setting out to become the official representative of the Pennsylvania colonists to the mother country, but he would become even more important than the ones who sent him or those who would receive him realized.

Benjamin Franklin was a man of the American people. He represented American colonial feeling about events that were occurring in Britain and in the American colonies. At the moment of his departure he held a position that might be roughly compared to that of an ambassador, if a colony can be said to have an ambassador to its mother country. At first, he represented Pennsylvania and then all the American colonies in the only external relationship that was of any importance to them—the relationship with Mother England.

The relationship between the colonies and the mother country existed on several levels. This was the period of the French and Indian War, and the Earl of Loudoun was assembling a fleet to send against the French. Loudoun was charged with the defense of the colonies or, rather, with the defeat of the French, who were coming down from French Canada. But Loudoun would not take the responsibility for the defense of any single colony. He told the governor of Pennsylvania that he would not spare one soldier to defend the Pennsylvania borders against attack. Defense of the borders, he said, was the task of the inhabitants of the colony.

In London, Franklin was in a remarkably strong position for an American. Generally speaking, the upper-class Englishmen looked down upon the colonial people. It was difficult, however, for any but the snobs to disregard Franklin. He was a member of the Royal Society. He had already contributed more to science and to letters than most of the best brains of English society. His work with electricity was well known and much appreciated by students of natural science all over the world. His reputation for scientific and cultural works made it possible for him to take up effectively his role as diplomat.

Franklin believed that the Pennsylvania Assembly and all the assemblies of the colonies were largely self-governing bodies. He felt that the assemblies should enact the laws the people wanted. Then, usually through his governor, the king would give consent to these laws. But once the laws were made, they could not be changed arbitrarily, nor could the king or the governor make laws without the consent of the assemblies.

Franklin called on, and made his views known to Lord George Grenville—a British statesman who later became prime minister (1763–1765)—who disagreed with him. According to Grenville, the king and his council were legislators for all the colonies, and their instructions were the highest laws in the colonies. The Privy Council was the last resort of the colonies when they had difficulties, and the assemblies had no real power.

Because of various delays, Franklin spent five years in London, always expecting that in a month or a few months he would be able to set sail for home. He occupied the time in philosophical studies and discussion, scientific research and talk, and with his writing. His duties as agent consisted largely of stating the position of the colonials, and then waiting interminably while the English politicians avoided the issues.

11

A handful of English political leaders thought that the people of America should be treated as full citizens of England in order to keep American goodwill. One such leader, Attorney General Charles Pratt, told Franklin that some day the Americans would attempt to become independent. Franklin did not believe this statement and refused to consider it. He said, "No such idea was ever entertained by the Americans, nor will any such ever enter their heads, unless you grossly abuse them."

One could not say yet that Franklin was acting as official representative of all the American colonies, although in his mission to London, Franklin was the representative of the highest type of American colonial and was regarded as "Mr. America." But Franklin was more than a representative of Pennsylvania. He tried to remove the prejudices of the English ruling class against *all* Americans, using methods he had found effective in public life in the colonies. He turned to the press, writing many letters to the editors of various newspapers. Sometimes he paid to have these published.

But for the most part, Franklin represented the interests of Pennsylvania, and functioned as its unofficial ambassador. Several outstanding quarrels were to be decided, involving, on the one side, the crown and the proprietors of the colony (the Penns) and, on the other, the colonists.

In the end, Franklin effected a compromise on the matter of taxation of the Penn lands. The Penns agreed to be taxed on surveyed lands but not on the wild, unsurveyed lands. The victory was a real one for the colonial assembly, because the assembly won the right to tax land in the province without the feudal exemptions that had existed previously. One might say that this victory represented the first accomplishment of an American policy.

While Benjamin Franklin was living in London, the North

American continent was undergoing great changes. The British captured Fort Duquesne and Louisbourg in 1758. The next year, General Wolfe captured Quebec from the French. In 1760, all of Canada surrendered, and the British were forced to make a vital decision: would they keep Canada, with all the territory and the responsibility that involved, or would they give it back to the French?

For a time there was question whether the British would keep Canada or the important West Indian sugar island of Guadeloupe. Many important people in London preferred the rich sugar island to the cold and wild land north of the American colonies.

Franklin began a campaign in London for the retention of Canada by the English. He said the American colonies would never be secure as long as potential enemies existed on any side. He predicted that some day the English colonies in North America would be more important in terms of wealth and population than the British Isles.

In the summer of 1762, Franklin returned to America, his mission satisfactorily concluded. But in the fall of 1764, he again set out for London.

One might say that Benjamin Franklin left America to travel once more as ambassador of Pennsylvania to the mother country. Officially, his position was not even as dignified as that of ambassador of Pennsylvania, but, he was becoming the elder statesman and spokesman for all the American colonies.

In England, Franklin set about his new mission—to secure the freedom of the colony of Pennsylvania from the Penns, to whom the land had been granted so long before. Pennsylvania occupied a unique position as a proprietary colony, and there were many thoughtful men in London who believed the colony ought to be sold back to the crown. But the demands of the Pennsylvanians for freedom angered a royalist faction, which believed the common people had too many rights and that the colonists in America were becoming entirely too independent.

Then the Stamp Act was born.

Early in 1765, the English Parliament considered a new idea in dealing with the colonies of North America. Spurred by the leaders who needed money to pay for the war against France, Parliament set a direct tax on the American colonies. The new tax was to be placed on newspapers, almanacs, pamphlets, legal documents, insurance policies, ship's papers, licenses, and even playing cards. It was to be collected by sale of tax stamps, which would be fixed to these papers.

Theoretically, the receipts of this tax were to be paid out of the royal treasury for the defense and maintenance of the American colonies. But the Americans contended that the receipts were used to support the English government, not the American government. They said they had already paid their share of the war costs.

Thus, *all* the English colonists in America were faced with a common problem—for the first time, one might say. The Stamp Act was a general tax on the colonies. The colonists in the North and South, much as they differed on almost all other matters, were in complete agreement that it was a dangerous and hurtful tax.

Annoyed about taxes and about American attitudes, the English rulers were not willing to listen to Benjamin Franklin's pleas for a change in the form of government in Pennsylvania. The opinion in many circles was that the Americans were becoming far too difficult to manage and must be stepped on firmly if the colonies were not to get entirely out of hand. The English also felt that their own taxes were far too high and that the Americans were not paying enough for their own support.

The British rulers and Franklin did not realize immediately (for they were far away from America and events were moving swiftly) that the negative reaction to the Stamp Act came from the common people more than from the educated and wealthy who dominated the assemblies or served as officials of the colonial governments. The people said the act was an outrage, a direct tax laid on them by Britain's Parliament and not by their own legislators.

In October, 1765, nine colonies sent representatives to New York as delegates to what became known as the Stamp Act Congress. The delegates reached a wide area of agreement. In November, when the stamps reached America, they were generally boycotted. Many businessmen refused to use the stamps, and soon Britain's businessmen discovered that trade with the American colonies was cut in half.

Franklin began working for the repeal of the Stamp Act. He called on members of both houses of Parliament. Soon he was known throughout England as the foremost advocate of repeal of this law. Franklin convinced William Pitt and Edmund Burke, powerful men in Parliament, but he did not convince the king and his friends. And George III was determined that he should rule as king. King and Parliament resented the complaints of the Americans.

The law was repealed in 1766 and Franklin became the acknowledged hero of the repeal. But he was not nearly so pleased at the repeal as his compatriots were. Franklin wanted real union, which included representation of Americans in Parliament. The repeal of this law was a sorry substitute for union, in Franklin's opinion, and he came to fear that the union would never materialize.

"The Parliament here do at present think too highly of themselves to admit representatives from us, if we should ask it; and, when they will be desirous of granting it, we shall think too highly of ourselves to accept of it," he wrote a

15

friend that spring, a wise remark about the relationships of colonies and mother countries that was to have meaning still in the twentieth century.

So great was Benjamin Franklin's reputation in the colonies that he became the closest thing to an agent-general or general representative that the colonies might have in England. In 1768, he was chosen agent for Georgia, then agent for New Jersey, and, in 1770, agent for Massachusetts as well. In his biography of Franklin, Carl Van Doren said that if the revolution had not come when it did, Franklin would have been agent-general for the colonies and that in effect he *was* agent-general, which was as close to a foreign minister as the American colonies might have.

Franklin had a lofty concept of the relationship of America to England. The colonies, he said, represented an independent state, or set of states, entitled to make their own laws under the sovereignty of the crown.

George III was very much opposed to this idea. Franklin dealt with this royal attitude in a monograph he wrote for the *Public Advertiser* of London, a satire called *Rules by which a Great Empire May Be Reduced to a Small One.* In that satire he said, "Never believe that the discontents of the colonies are general or in any way justified. Listen to all the governors say, to nothing you hear from the friends of the people."

That ironic advice was to be taken seriously by a humorless English government.

Franklin was a long-suffering man. He remained in England, doing his work, but becoming more and more convinced that there was no hope of healing the rupture between the colonies and England. In England, Franklin was regarded as the example of, if not the reason for, most of the troubles between America and England.

Franklin resigned as the Massachusetts assembly's representative, saying he could do no further good for the province. He wrote to friends in Boston, deploring the Boston Tea Party. The king and Lord North listened to Governor Hutchinson, not to Franklin, and soon Parliament passed a number of restrictive measures, closing the port of Boston until the tea was paid for, cutting the power of the Massachusetts assembly, and ordering that officials who broke the law be tried in England rather than in Massachusetts.

Massachusetts, her ports closed, asked for help from other colonies. They responded, acting in common for the common good.

Parliament unwisely tried to keep the colonies from manufacturing cloth by prohibiting the export of tools. Other unpleasant restrictions were put into force. The committees of correspondence of the various colonies, which had been formed to keep legislators aware of what was happening in the North and South, grew ever more active.

Franklin stayed on in England, awaiting the results of a Congress called by Virginia for May, 1774, at Philadelphia. Franklin hoped that the colonies would show unity and steadfastness. If the colonies started a general boycott of goods from England, the North ministry would fall, and Franklin expected that friends of his, in the opposition, would come to power in England.

Franklin was pressed by friends of the English government to draw up a plan of reconciliation. He saw no hope in it but he did draw up a plan, listing 17 points that must be resolved. But even as Franklin drew up this plan, affairs were moving to a climax in America.

Franklin's plan called for compromises on both sides. The colonists must pay for the tea destroyed in the Boston Tea Party, but the act laying a duty on tea must be repealed. The

Navigation Acts were to be repealed, and the right to regulate navigation turned over to the colonial governments. Customs officers were to be Americans, not Englishmen. Judges and governors were to be paid by the colonial assemblies. Parliament's threat to try Americans for treason under an old law of King Henry VIII was to be disavowed. American admiralty courts were to have equal powers with those of England. Only the colonial legislatures were to have the right to impose quartering of troops on the colonists.

In September, 1774, however, the First Continental Congress met in Philadelphia, offering plans of its own and condemning harsh British laws. Thirteen Parliamentary acts passed between 1763 and 1774 were criticized as unjust.

On December 18, after the Continental Congress had adjourned, a petition from that body to the king was brought to London, and Franklin and the other colonial agents were asked to present it. Franklin and two other agents presented the petition to Lord Dartmouth, Secretary of State. Dartmouth received them graciously and gave them hope that the king might receive their petition in a friendly manner.

In January, on the specific invitation of one of the lords, Franklin went to the House of Lords to be present when a measure of reconciliation was brought in. Several lords spoke for the Americans as defending all English freedom, but most members were not listening. In the end, 68 lords and bishops voted against the measure; only 18 voted for it.

Another plan for reconciliation was offered by Lord Chatham. But Lord Sandwich, who hated Franklin and America, claimed it was Franklin's, not Chatham's plan. Chatham admitted that Franklin had advised him, calling him "an honor not to the English nation only but to human nature."

After this meeting, Lord North decided to send 6,000 men to America to suppress the "rebellion." Franklin became furious, and finally gave up hope altogether. He went home, arriving at Philadelphia on May 5, just in time to learn of the outbreak of fighting at Lexington and Concord, where the minutemen fought the British. On May 6, Franklin was chosen by the Pennsylvania assembly to attend the Second Continental Congress, which was to meet in Philadelphia in four days.

If there was a single man in the colonies at this time who knew the temper of America and the temper of England, it was Benjamin Franklin. He was the most honored figure in all the American colonies.

The Infant Republic

When Benjamin Franklin returned to Philadelphia in 1775, he was convinced that the American colonies must seek and find independence. He was the oldest delegate to the Continental Congress, but there was no more determined revolutionary there than he, nor one so wise in the ways of the English crown and its servants.

Not all the colonists—by far—wanted independence. Perhaps the best illustration of the mixed states of mind of Americans came almost immediately on Franklin's return to America. Franklin met with his son, William, then royal governor of New Jersey, and Joseph Galloway, his most trusted confidant in the Pennsylvania assembly, and tried to persuade them to join him in supporting independence. Neither man would support a break with the mother country. Joseph Galloway eventually went to England to pledge his loyalty to the crown. William refused to follow his father and became head of the Tory organization in New York after the British captured the city and made an English stronghold of it.

As a rebelling member of the new Congress, Franklin joined Benjamin Harrison, John Dickinson, Thomas Johnson, and John Jay to form the Committee of Secret Correspondence, a new committee authorized by the Continental Congress. This committee was the first all-American committee on foreign affairs, the forerunner of the American Department of State. Its major responsibility was to establish correspondence with friends of America in other parts of the world.

If Franklin could not convince his son and his political lieutenant, he did convince dozens of other young men that the British rulers regarded privilege as a right, and that the colonies would not secure the freedom of action they now demanded as *their* right. The British government had declared the Americans to be rebels.

The committee was soon in touch with Achard de Bonvouloir, a secret agent of the king of France, who came to Philadelphia and through the offices of a French bookseller made himself known to Benjamin Franklin. Agent Bonvouloir represented no less an authority than the Comte de Vergennes, the French foreign minister. He had been sent to America to carry the word that France would like to see the American colonies gain their independence and then convert their trade from England to France. (Until this time, trade between the colonies and industrial nations other than England was virtually nonexistent; it had been an aspect of colonization that *all* the trade of a colony was carried out with the mother country, to the benefit of the mother country's treasury and her merchants. In the beginning, the establishment of fortunes from trade was the single greatest impetus to development of colonies, although some colonies were formed originally for religious or political reasons.) Soon Bonvouloir and the members of the committee were meeting

21

at night in sessions so secret that each man came alone to the meeting place, having made sure he was not followed.

In December, 1775, the secret committee on foreign affairs convinced the French agent that a declaration of American independence was a certainty (although it would not be made for another six months) and Bonvouloir informed his foreign minister of this.

In December, 1775, Franklin wrote to Don Gabriel of Bourbon, a Spanish prince, to ask Spain to assist the American colonies, particularly in view of the mutual interest the Americans and the Spanish had in Florida. Franklin also wrote to friends in Holland and in France, sending them copies of the proceedings of the Continental Congress, with the definite purpose of enlisting sympathy and assistance.

Franklin asked other friends abroad for reports on the chances of foreign alliances and to secure the services of military engineers, who were badly needed by the colonies. After all, the defenses of the colonies—gunpowder, the guns, and the knowledge of fortifications—were largely in the hands of the British. If the colonies were to rebel, they must find supplies of powder, must make their own munitions, and must learn to build their own forts.

In 1776, Congress contracted with French companies to supply munitions in exchange for goods from the United States. This was a measure of definite independence, or treasonable action, depending on the point of view. Never before had an American body gone so far as to contract with foreign governments for materials with which to war on the government of the king.

In March, 1776, Congress voted to send Silas Deane to France as its representative, or ambassador. Deane went off armed with instructions written carefully by Benjamin Franklin. One might say, then, that Franklin was acting as foreign minister for Congress.

In March, 1776, Franklin was asked to go to Canada. American military men had attacked and captured Montreal and threatened Quebec City. But the Americans behaved so badly in Canada that the French Catholic people of Quebec turned against them; and instead of winning the Canadian colonies to the American side in this fight against England, quite the reverse was happening.

In 1774, in order to punish the American colonies and put a carrot before the nose of the French in North America, Parliament had passed the Quebec Act, which guaranteed the French freedom to practice the Catholic religion and their own judicial code, which was quite different from that of the English. The law also extended the boundaries of Quebec south to the Ohio and west to the Mississippi River, which took in portions of territory claimed by Massachusetts and several other colonies. The American colonies had responded with ill-temper and abuse against the French Catholics, and the French had not forgotten it. Had the American army behaved properly in Canada, the story might have been different, and so might the threads of American history.

By the time Franklin came to Quebec, however, the cause was lost, and he sensed it. The French were anti-American. There were only 400 English Protestants in the province, and most of them were Loyalists. Franklin learned of the British reinforcement of Quebec City, and came to the immediate conclusion that the American army would be driven out of Canada before summer, which it was. Franklin went home to Philadelphia and Congress.

After the Declaration of American Independence in July, 1776, Franklin continued to be the guiding figure in American relations with foreign peoples and governments. He was sick a good deal that summer, however, and much of the work was turned over to others. Lord Howe, who had conducted private conversations with Franklin in London, tried to reach the colonies and effect reconciliation through Franklin again, but it was impossible; and after consulting with Congress, Franklin told him so.

"Long did I endeavor," Franklin wrote Lord Howe, "with unfeigned and unwearied zeal to preserve from breaking that fine and noble china vase the British Empire; for I knew that, once being broken, the separate parts could not retain even their shares of the strength and value that existed in the whole, and that a perfect reunion of those parts could scarce ever be hoped for."

In September, Franklin, John Adams, and Edward Rutledge of South Carolina went to meet with Howe on Staten Island, a meeting that ended in failure. The same month, Franklin received a long letter from France indicating strong interest in a Franco-American alliance, and he was asked to go as a commissioner to France to further such a plan. In November, Franklin and the other commissioners were in France, prepared to negotiate a treaty, and fully empowered to do so by Congress. Franklin had been sent to France because the government of Louis XVI was potentially the strongest ally that America could have, and it was important to America that she receive strong and immediate aid. Yet as far as his direct control, or influence on the control, of American foreign policy, Benjamin Franklin stepped into the background with his removal to the important post in Paris. As the months wore on, the American Congress in Philadelphia was forced to make decisions regarding matters that affected relationships with nations other than France, and since Franklin was not present, other men's ideas were adopted.

One might say that American foreign policy as such became official in the Articles of Confederation and Perpetual Union, proposed in July, 1776, and finally ratified on March 1, 1781.

With Franklin in Paris, a new committee was formed. Still referred to as the Committee of Secret Correspondence, the new committee undertook the general management of American foreign relations in Franklin's absence.

But with Franklin away, the committee declined in importance. When he was chairman, all the younger men gave way before his undoubtedly superior knowledge and experience. Once he had left, Congress jealously kept to itself the responsibility for relationships with outsiders, regarding the function as so important that special committees were chosen to handle each question as it arose.

In the spring of 1777 it became apparent that too many committees did not make for efficiency of management, and as negotiations of various kinds must be carried on with many foreigners, some order was needed. On April 17, Congress regularized the secret committee and gave it the title Committee for Foreign Affairs. Franklin being absent, the members were Benjamin Harrison, Robert Morris, Thomas Hayward, Jr., and James Lovell.

The first secretary of the committee was Thomas Paine, who had risen rapidly to national prominence after publication a few years earlier of his *Common Sense*, which was so succinct and persuasive in its arguments against reunion with England. Paine's function was to manage the affairs of the committee. He was paid $70 per month. The committee's task was to keep the various American agents abroad up to date about American affairs. Congress was so jealous of its prerogatives and so unsure of any of its members and servants that the committee membership was constantly changed.

The Committee for Foreign Affairs was seldom allowed to function in foreign affairs. Less than a month after it was formed, when an occasion came up to manage some business between Congress and the government of Portugal, a special committee of Congress was assigned to the task. The problem was to inquire into various national customs regarding neutrality of nations. The matter had been brought to the attention of Congress by a ruling of the king of Portugal forbidding his subjects from entering American ports and forcing those subjects in American ports to depart. What Congress wanted to know was whether the king was not siding with the American enemies.

The Committee for Foreign Affairs did so little that most of its work is hardly worth recounting. Franklin and his associates in Paris were able to report, at the end of 1777, that they had made good progress toward bringing France into the war on the side of America. In February, 1778, a treaty was signed in Paris to establish diplomatic relations between France and America. The French sent an ambassador, Conrad Alexander Gerard, to the United States. This action made the orderly management of foreign relations essential.

One of the first questions that had to be answered by the new government was how to deal with foreign representatives when they arrived in America, the question of protocol. A new committee was established to make recommendations, but the committee became simply a figurehead. When the French minister Gerard's first audience was held, on August 6, 1778, the members of the committee participated as ordinary members of Congress.

The matter of foreign policy was second in importance only to war itself. Great Britain certainly possessed the men and facilities to win a war on the American continent, or at least to capture all the ports and cities and establish a strong occupation. If the colonies did not secure allies, eventually the revolutionaries would be forced to surrender. There were many Loyalists and many only half-convinced supporters of independence in the colonies even in 1778. Victory for the colonies depended on what allies Congress might be able to attract. Besides French aid, alliances with various other nations, Spain, in particular, were eagerly sought. The basic foreign policy of the burgeoning nation now became one of friendly alliance with nations other than England and promise of trade with those European countries which would help America in this hour of great need.

But the manner of carrying on these relations was as irregular as it could be, with the entire membership of Congress insisting on participating in important affairs.

Even in 1779, it was Congress that began discussions of a treaty of peace to be negotiated with Great Britain, and early in August a committee of five members of Congress was selected especially for this task. The Committee of Foreign Affairs was not used. In 1779, Thomas Paine was dismissed as secretary of the committee for making public an official, if unimportant, matter. Yet Paine's dismissal was not the reason for the committee's lack of power; Congress was simply not organized in a fashion that would permit the establishment of a permanent committee to handle so delicate a subject as foreign affairs.

One reason for the committee's failures was the inability or unwillingness of its members to undertake the major job they were assigned. The committee's prime task was to keep the American representatives abroad informed as to the work of Congress, the state of mind of the people at home, and the progress of the war. The committee simply did not do its job. Its members were jealous of position more than anything else, as can be seen in a letter from committee member James Lovell to Arthur Lee in August, 1779.

> But there is really no such thing, as a committee of foreign affairs existing—no secretary or clerk further than I persevere to be one or the other. The books and the papers of that extinguished body lay yet on the table of Congress, or rather are locked up in the secretary's private box. There was a motion, as I have before told you, to choose a new committee; the house would not so insult *me*.

By the end of 1780, all the American envoys overseas were thoroughly disgusted with the Committee on Foreign Affairs. "One good private correspondent would be worth twenty standing committees, made of the wisest heads in America, for the purpose of intelligence," wrote John Jay. The system of managing foreign affairs was a total failure.

In January, 1781, the Continental Congress realized that a change must be made, and it was proposed that a Department of Foreign Affairs be established, in a resolution that noted "the delay and indecision" in the current way of managing foreign affairs. Some members of Congress wanted a strong foreign affairs committee, with the President as a permanent member. Others did not wish to give any one man so much power, and in the continuing jealousies among the colonies this position won out. The wheels were set in motion, but they turned very slowly, and it was not until August that Robert R. Livingston of New York was elected the first secretary of the new Department of Foreign Affairs.

One of the Livingston's first actions was to inform Foreign Minister Vergennes of France of his appointment. Next he informed the four American ministers abroad: Benjamin Franklin in Paris, John Adams in The Hague, Francis Dana in Russia, and John Jay in Spain. There were various consuls and agents in foreign ports, also, but these four men had the grave responsibility of securing support and financial assistance for the American revolution.

Congress obviously intended that the new department be an important agency and not, as the old committee, just a repository of unwanted correspondence. Secretary Livingston received the very high salary of $4,000 a year, and was given two undersecretaries who were paid well enough by the standards of the day at $700 and $800 a year.

But Congress was not willing to give the new department the authority needed to conduct foreign relations on a sensible level. Most members of Congress were very careful not to commit their own colonies to any more joint action than was absolutely essential. Each representative considered his own colony to be an independent state. It was apparent, of course, that the colonies would have to band together to conduct a general post office, to raise armies and conduct war, if necessary, and to present a united face to the world through the Secretariat of Foreign Affairs. That was why they had been willing to form the Secretariat. But when it came down to details, that was another matter.

Secretary Livingston was an able and dedicated man. He was a lawyer, and had served on the old Foreign Affairs Committee of the Continental Congress. He was a good friend of Benjamin Franklin's, too. From the beginning, however, he was placed in a strange and puzzling position.

Congress authorized Livingston to attend their sessions, but he was not given access to the congressional records, which were secret. Congress also continued the practice of making direct contact with foreign diplomats, sometimes without telling Livingston what the congressional committee involved was doing. (Eventually, Congress would even betray the confidence of America's French allies by opening negotiations for a separate peace with England.)

After six months of such confusion, Secretary Livingston complained in a letter to Congress President Samuel Huntington that Congress had failed to consider many important matters when the Secretariat was established. He felt his letters to the American diplomats abroad ought to represent the thinking of Congress, but since he was not given access to the records he did not always know how Congress felt. Also, he had no specific authority to ask questions in Congress, and he wanted such authority in order to inform himself. He had no authority to act on unimportant matters, such as applications for aid from Americans in trouble, claims against ships taken as prizes, and other day-to-day matters that involved relations between Americans and governments of other countries.

Livingston reported that he had been carrying on such business, even without this authority, but he did not like it. Nor was his staff large enough, he said. His two assistants simply could not keep up with the work. Five copies had to be made of every foreign letter and paper, and this kept his men busy. He was behind in copying such things as letters already received, secret congressional journals, journals of the diplomats abroad, and extracts in congressional files that concerned foreign relations. The government of the future had to have all this information if American foreign policy was to have any continuity, and he was now a full year behind in the paperwork.

Livingston also said he needed at least one interpreter for his department to carry on relations with the French. He needed more clerks. And he needed a personal secretary.

When Secretary Livingston's letter was read, and it was made clear that he sought clarification and authority that he was unwilling to usurp, Congress was swift to act. An inventory was made of the books and papers kept in the office of foreign affairs. Conferences were held with Livingston, after which a three-member congressional committee drew up a report recommending a number of changes in procedure. More than that, the Secretary to the United States of America for the Department of Foreign Affairs was given more authority to match his responsibility.

Congress said the Secretary was to keep all the books and records relating to his department. He was to carry on diplomatic correspondence with American ministers abroad and with foreign ministers in America. (Congress here showed its awareness that it had been stepping into the Secretary's bailiwick.) Of course, the Secretary was to be responsible to Congress. Matters relating to treaties were to be submitted for Congressional approval before action or transmittal. The Secreatary was also given another power that might seem odd today but in 1782 was not odd at all. He was made responsible for correspondence with governors and presidents of the various states. He was to give these people information about his department's activities, and to state any complaints made against any of the states by foreign powers.

The Secretary was also to continue to attend sessions of Congress. He could give information to Congress and answer objections. He was to start collecting political and economic information about other countries, as soon as possible.

The number of his clerks was not specified, which meant he could hire more; and he was given a private secreatry with a salary of $1,000 a year. It was also proposed that he be given a seat in Congress, but that provision was stricken from the law, along with Livingston's plea for an official interpreter.

With these changes, the Department of Foreign Affairs came of age, with only one peculiar restriction. The Secretary was still dependent on the will of Congress in many small ways.

For instance, Congress watched the new department carefully. In the summer of 1782 a special committee investigated the Department of Foreign Affairs; it reported to Congress that everything was quite in order. Nonetheless, in the autumn of 1782, Robert Livingston was unhappy. He had been chosen chancellor of the State of New York, an administrative-judicial post that took more and more of his time, and he found that the office of Secretary of Foreign Affairs had become far too difficult. He was spending $3,000 more per year on the job than he was getting in salary. He had many social responsibilities, entertaining foreign guests and bringing them together with members of Congress. Each American minister abroad was receiving a salary of more than $11,000 a year, to do much the same on the other end of the line, so it was no wonder that the Secretary had financial difficulties. Livingston let it be known that if his salary were made large enough to live properly, he would stay. A bill was introduced in Congress to raise the Secretary's pay, but it was rejected.

Livingston decided to retire at the end of 1782, but was persuaded to stay on in office while Congress looked for a successor. None was found by May, and Livingston sent a formal letter of resignation.

This first Secretary of Foreign Affairs had established a number of important precedents in the American conduct of foreign relations. Until the colonies rebelled openly, foreigners had sometimes been hired to represent American interests abroad. Some of the agents of the colonies were Englishmen. Livingston advised that only American citizens should be appointed to foreign diplomatic posts. He insisted, to the chagrin of some ministers and consuls, that they must report in detail and regularly on their activities. Along with Benjamin Franklin, he insisted that the American representatives abroad must have decent pay.

All during the revolution, Congress continued to be jealous of its power. James Madison later wrote that he believed Livingston had resigned because Congress was always meddling in minor affairs. The men of Congress were sorry to lose him, for he had taught them one important lesson. He had insisted that American affairs must be conducted on the basis of accepted international law. Before Livingston came to office, there were many in Congress who believed that the nation need not be bound by international law. Franklin and Livingston, together, won the victory that brought regular foreign relations between the sturggling revolutionary government and other countries, and created respect for the Americans for observing the forms.

When Livingston quit his office, in June, 1783, he sealed up his official papers and turned them over to the Secretary of Congress. Lewis Morris, the first undersecretary of the department, was left in charge of affairs. But without the department's papers and without any authority to act, he soon became disgusted and resigned.

For two months the department was thoroughly disrupted. Then Congress decided to examine the papers and discover what action might be necessary. It also decided that it was of the highest importance to find a new Secretary of Foreign Affairs.

John Jay, minister to Spain, agreed to take the post. He had been suggested for the assignment by Livingston, but, since he was in the middle of treaty negotiations with Spain, he had not wanted to leave Europe. He came back to the United States, and took office in September, 1784.

Congress, mindful of Livingston's reason for resignation, made a motion to give Secretary Jay $1,000 a year more than Livingston's $4,000 salary. But the conservative guardians of the treasury in Congress won the day, and the motion was not passed.

Jay gave signs of becoming most impatient with Congress. He wrote Congress for specific instructions on the conduct of his office. He insisted on choosing his own clerks, and he wanted an interpreter. Congress insisted that letters from foreign lands be communicated to Congress—and when the Congressmen received some letters, in foreign languages, it was not long before they authorized an interpreter for John Jay.

Shortly after John Jay came into office, the American government was moved to New York City. Jay's first office was in a room of the New York City Hall, which Congress had taken over as a temporary meeting place. In April, 1785, Congress leased a building at the southeast corner of Broad and Pearl Streets. The Department of Foreign Affairs occupied two rooms in that building, one for Secretary Jay and one for his assistant and a clerk.

The members of Congress began to realize that if they wanted to keep good men in the office of the Secretary of Foreign Affairs, they must relinquish some of their day-to-day auhority. Even so, Congress was very slow to give up power.

In the days of the Revolution, treaties with foreign powers had been made by special ministers abroad, under specific instructions from Congress. The first such responsibility to be given to the Secretary of Foreign Affairs came to John Jay in 1786, when Spain and America were talking about a boundary treaty to define the limits of Florida and the American claims.

Secretary Jay was forthright and businesslike. Since he did not much care for the limited power that Congress had given him, he called the attention of Congress to the situation in a letter. Would not Congress appoint a committee, he asked, to instruct him on every point in the proposed treaty?

Congress understood his request. In August, 1786, Secretary Jay was given power to "treat, adjust, conclude and sign with Don Diego de Gardoqui" a boundary treaty. To be sure, Secretary Jay had to inform Congress of the propositions made to him before he agreed to any of them. Congress was not about to allow the Secretary of Foreign Affairs to actually negotiate a treaty and to present an accomplished fact. But Secretary Jay had again called attention to the difficulties under which he worked. Congress was learning something about the needs of a civil government and the manner in which foreign affairs must be carried out if they were to be conducted sensibly.

Congress continued to regard its powers jealously, and Jay was politician enough not to annoy the congressmen unnecessarily. As a citizen of New York, he was called upon to attend the Poughkeepsie Convention of 1788, at which the representatives of New York had to vote to accept or reject the proposed federal Constitution. Instead of accepting the invitation immediately, as he wanted to do, Secretary Jay felt sufficiently weighed by his responsibilities to ask the pleasure of Congress in the matter. Congress appreciated this courtesy and gave Jay permission to attend the convention.

In the summer of 1788, the expiring Congress of the federated republic made one last report on the Department of Foreign Affairs before allowing the new Congress to take office under the new Constitution. The reporting committee found a government department much enlarged in responsibility and scope from that headed by Robert Livingston. Secretary Jay had been able to employ enough clerks to run the department with skill and thoroughness. Daily dispatches were entered by hand in a minute book, and these were copied into a journal, kept in two folio volumes. The Secretary wrote letters regularly to the foreign missions, and these were recorded in a special book. If there were secret matters to be discussed, parts of the letters were recorded in cipher.

The department kept files of correspondence wih foreign ministers, reports to Congress, records of all negotiations, passports for vessels, letters of commission to foreign ministers, accounts, congressional acts relating to the department, and records of the previous correspondence of ministers. It had Minister Dana's leters from 1780–1783 from Russia, those of H. Laurens and J. Laurens to Russia and Versailles; five volumes of John Adams' letters from Spain, and several other volumes.

When the committee made its study of the department in the summer of 1788, Secretary Jay was busy negotiating with the Spanish about border problems. So complex were these negoiations that one full volume of papers in the office was devoted to them. But an expiring Congress could not continue to take responsibility for a treaty or to lead the Spanish into thinking that the actions sanctioned under the Articles of Confederation would be acceptable under the Constitution, and so a special committee which considered the subject recommended that Secretary Jay stop negotiations. The matter was to be referred to the new federal government, which would assemble in March, 1789.

So the loose confederation came to an end. One major reason for the banding together of the federated states in union was the need to conduct foreign relations as one state. England, France, Spain, and the Netherlands had all brought up this delicate subject, and had made the representatives of the Continental Congress aware of the weakness of the 13 colonies unless they joined together. The matters of common defense and common road systems and common money and banking were all important. But the most persuasive argument was that union was needed simply to carry on day-to-day relationships with the manufacturing countries of the world which had to supply the needs of growing, agricultural America. The need for a united foreign policy was evident before the day of the Declaration of Independence, and creation of a system under which united foreign policy could be worked out and enforced was essential to the new nation.

The Virginia Dynasty

One of the strengths of the new Constitution was the broad wording which established principles of government but left the details to Congress and other arms of government.

The creation of an executive branch was established in the Constitution, for example, but the creation of the various departments was left up to the President and Congress.

In 1789, the new Congress of the United States set about electing a chief executive. In April, George Washington was elected President and John Adams was elected Vice-President. When Washington was inaugurated as the first President of the United States, he had no specific executive departments at his disposal.

The three most needed departments were those of Foreign Affairs, Treasury, and War. These areas represented the basic reasons for the Union.

Questions concerning the Secretary of Foreign Affairs were taken up first. How should he be appointed? How should he serve? How could he be removed?

These questions, which had to be hammered out in debate among members of the two new Houses of Congress, were settled in July: The Secretary of Foreign Affairs should be appointed by the President. He should serve at the President's pleasure, and a chief clerk should have custody of all papers in case of a vacancy in the office. He could be removed at the President's request.

However, a new problem arose. Some members of Congress saw the need for a Home Department, which would see to the execution of the federal laws, keep the seals, check on laws of the various states—to see that they did not conflict with federal laws—keep archives, conduct surveys and the census, and do a dozen other jobs related to the federalization of government.

Many said the work could be done by the Secretary of Foreign Affairs and by the judiciary, a view which became popular. Most congressmen began to believe that the Department of Foreign Affairs was not too busy to handle all the work that did not normally fall within the scopes of the Treasury and War Departments.

In mid-September, after much debate it was decided to try to change the name of the Department of Foreign Affairs to the Department of *State*. Added would be the duties of recording laws of Congress, sending copies to the various states, and keeping the laws on file. The new department would be the custodian of the seal of the United States and fix the seal to all government commissions on the order of the President. The Secretary of State would also undertake the duties of the old Secretary of Congress, keeping congressional documents and records, as well as such duties of the Treasury and War Departments as the President might wish to give him.

The continuity of government was maintained by John Jay.

Since he had been Congress's Secretary of Foreign Affairs, and since he was first Secretary of Foreign Affairs for the new government, he became first Secretary of State, with the understanding that he was simply holding the office until President Washington appointed a new man. (Jay wanted to be Chief Justice of the Supreme Court.)

By fall, 1789, the department was complete. The Secretary of State was to receive only $3,500 instead of the $4,000 that the Secretary of Foreign Affairs had begun with, but times were hard in America and the new money was worth far more than the old Continenal currency.

The Department of State was not much larger than Jay's old department had been. It consisted of the Secretary, an undersecretary, or chief clerk, two clerks, a French interpreter, a doorkeeper and a messenger. But there were a few new allowances, such as $150 a year to pay for other interpretation when needed and $200 for office rent.

Historically speaking then, John Jay was the first Secretary of State. But in terms of effective policy and development of the office, the first Secretary was Thomas Jefferson.

President Washington was looking for distinguished men to serve in his executive department. Jefferson had served well in many high offices, and had distinguished himself particularly as commissioner to formulate the peace treaty with England after the revolution, and as successor to Benjamin Franklin in the very important mission to France.

Jefferson really did not wish to become Secretary of State, and he told friends this. President Washington wrote Jefferson, asking him to take the office, and Jefferson agreed, but he did say that he would prefer to return to Paris as minister.

Because of the pressure of personal affairs at his estate, Monticello, and business in Richmond, Jefferson did not ac-

Thomas Jefferson

tually take office until the spring of 1790. Immediately, he faced a vexing problem:

Under John Jay, Henry Remson, Jr., had served as chief clerk, or Undersecretary of State, and he continued to handle the papers that concerned foreign affairs. When the new duties were given the office of Secretary of State, Jay had turned over the keeping of the seal and nonforeign-affairs papers to Roger Alden, who had been Deputy Secretary of Congress and was familiar with such material. So Jefferson now had two chief clerks, where the law provided for only one. Neither man was willing to step down. Jefferson solved the problem by retaining both at $800 a year each, and on June 4, 1790, Congress approved the irregular arrangement. Alden soon found the pay too low and quit. Jefferson then made Remson chief clerk and merged the duties of the office.

When Jefferson became Secretary, he realized that President Washington considered the conduct of foreign affairs to be one of his major responsibilities. Washington acted as his own Secretary of State in the sense that he evaluated much of the information as well as made the final decisions on foreign policy. Jefferson was quite amenable to this system, by which the first President of the United States established a precedent that many others were to follow.

John Jay had had much trouble with England during his tenure as Secretary of State. The English tended to sneer at the new nation, and placed many unpleasant restrictions on trade with the United States. The Americans protested about the slowness of the British in retreating from the northern outposts, as promised. The British replied that the Americans were not paying war damages, as promised, nor treating the Loyalists properly. Thomas Jefferson, who loved France, had grown to dislike England intensely, and he brought this attitude into office. He quarreled frequently in cabinet meetings with Alexander Hamilton, who loved England and disliked France, and they disagreed as much over foreign affairs as they did over the issue of whether the government should be centralized or decentralized.

The duties of the Department of State were now exactly what the President and Congress wanted them to be. The Department had been created as convenient bin-of-all-goods, and it so served. All civil appointments were made through the Secretary of State. The Secretary issued patents and carried out the census of 1790.

By 1790, the United States was ready to establish a real diplomatic and consular service. Ministers were serving, or preparing to serve, in London, Paris, Madrid, The Hague, and Lisbon. There were 16 consular offices abroad. All the diplomats were expected to send home reports once or twice a month, plus newspapers, magazines, and other papers that might be helpful to the United States government in understanding the world. Jefferson also laid down details about the duties of consular officials, pending congressional attention to his problem.

Jefferson's contribution to the operation of the Department of State was largely as administrator, regularizing the forms, and teaching those in the department the importance of a regular intelligence system about economic and political matters abroad.

He also established a principle of foreign affairs which was to be most important in the early days of the United States, the principle of recognition of foreign governments. When the French mobs overthrew the monarchy and established a republic, the United States was hard-pressed to determine what course to take regarding this overthrow of duly established authority. Jefferson laid down the principle that was followed by President Washington.

We surely cannot deny to any nation that right whereon our own government is founded—that everyone may govern itself according to whatever form it pleases and change these forms at its own will; and that it may transact its business wih foreign nations through whatever organ it thinks proper, whether king, convention, assembly, committee, president, or anything it may choose. The will of the nation is the only thing essential to be regarded.

In a cabinet argument with Alexander Hamilton, Jefferson held that no matter what the government of France might be, all the treaties previously made with France must be honored. Treaties were made between state and state, he said, and internal changes in government did not change the obligations.

When France went to war with England and Spain in the spring of 1793, the struggle caused untold embarrassment to the United States. The new nation had just emerged from long domination by England, and was still dominated in a trade sense by British capital. Many Americans desired a closer relationship than existed wih England and a more hands-off policy toward France—which had been America's ally in the Revolution—and toward Spain, which was America's neighbor to the south.

Hamilton was an Anglophile, and President Washington tended to agree more and more with Hamilton's points of view and less with Jefferson's, alhough Washington understood and respected Jefferson's basic position on the distribution of political power.

The United States in 1793 was party to a treaty of alliance with France that called for the United States to help France in case of war. Here was war between France and England. What was to be done?

Hamilton wanted an outright declaration of neutrality, and he wanted the United States to disavow all old treaties with Paris, on the ground that the Americans were not bound to respect the new government.

The United States was in no position to go to war with England, so even Jefferson agreed on neutrality. But he fought successfully for outright acceptance of the French minister Citizen Genêt and adherence to the old treaties.

Jefferson made one important declaration of American policy, a statement that was to guide Americans and foreigners from that time forward. Citizen Genêt proved to be a most difficult visitor. He conspired in the United States to try to bring America into France's war against England, and when he found that President Washington was standing firm for neutrality, he tried to go around Washington and deal directly with Congress. The precedent for this, of course, was the very different Continental Congress which had existed in the American Revolutionary days. Jefferson pointed out that the President of the United States was the only person to whom the foreign nations had any right to address themselves. He meant, of course, the President or his servants, the officials of the executive branch of the government. Foreigners would have to remember, he said, that they must listen only to the President to understand what was the will of the nation, because the President was specifically given the power to conduct the foreign relations of the nation.

It was an important declaration, although one that foreigners and Americans did not always recall or understand in the next 150 years. Yet, it was seldom threatened in application and never successfully circumvented. A hundred and seventy-four years after Jefferson's pronouncement, Secretary of State Dean Rusk was called upon to remind the world of this same policy, when he explained that foreigners must not listen to dissident Congressmen or to demonstrating crowds in the American streets when considering American foreign policy. The Jeffersonian principle had survived so long.

Jefferson quit the State Department over the French issue at the end of 1793, and Washington chose as his successor Edmund Randolph, a member of an important Virginia family. Randolph, who took office in January, 1794, was the victim of the political hysteria of his day. During this period, Hamilton was doing his best to achieve better relationships with Britain, and Randolph was continuing Jefferson's policy of trying to better relations with France. Citizen Genêt finally was replaced by a minister named Fauchet, who became friendly with Randolph. A letter from Fauchet to his home government was captured by a privateer and opened, and it indicated that Randolph was serving the ends of France more than those of the United States.

President Washington became furious and accused Randolph of improper conduct. He was convinced that Randolph had taken money from the French to do their bidding although no historical evidence was ever brought forth to prove this point. In August, 1795, Randolph resigned under a cloud of suspicion, the only Secretary of State ever to be accused of selling his services to another country.

Washington found it difficult in this second administration to find a Secretary of State from among his friends, because many of them had become alienated from his way of thinking. Patrick Henry, for example, believed the Washington administration was entirely too much dedicated to strong federal government.

For a time, Timothy Pickering, the Secretary of War, undertook the duties of the State Department. In 1796, a new War Secretary was appointed, and Pickering devoted his full efforts to affairs of state.

Edmund Randolph

Washington's years were years of delicate decisions. American relations with France and England were strained, particularly those with England, which insisted on searching American ships at sea. Washington had sent John Jay to negotiate a new trade treaty wih Britain. The treaty was debated thoroughly in Congress and in the nation. Eventually it was accepted, and it made relations between the United States and Britain tolerable for a time, although many out-standing matters, such as border problems, were yet to be resolved. Relations with France grew worse, for the United States was, in effect, supporting the British in the war against France by trading with Britain. Pickering, like many of the cabinet members of his day, would not have found war with the French revolutionaries unwelcome.

The second Washington administration expired, and, in 1797, President John Adams came to office. Pickering was kept on as Secretary of State in Adams' administration. Adams had a slightly different attitude toward the presidency and the responsibility for foreign policy. He was not nearly so inclined to consult with his cabinet before making deci-sions. He did not want war with France, and if Thomas Jeffer-son had not been elected Vice-President, Adams would have sent him on a mission of conciliation to Paris. But Jefferson could not be allowed out of the country since he was first in line of succession to the Presidency. The President decided on a special mission to establish a new climate in French-American relations.

Adams chose three envoys to go to Paris to try to retrieve a lost friendship for America. They were General Charles C. Pinckney, John Marshall—an outstanding Federalist who would later be Secretary of State—and Elbridge Gerry, a man of very liberal democratic leanings. Pickering's Francophobic views were known and he was not consulted.

Timothy Pickering

When the American envoys reached Paris, they discovered the climate was even worse than former Minister James Monroe had indicated. (Pickering had recalled Monroe as too friendly to France.) The French Directorate refused to receive the envoys, demanding first a redress of grievances. Pickering ordered the ministers to come home. Elbridge Gerry was persuaded to stay on as a private citizen by Foreign Minister Talleyrand. Gerry hoped to be able to bring about some understanding between the two governments.

A Quaker doctor named George Logan also visited France unofficially and came back to offer certain ideas to the State Department. When Pickering learned of these actions, he was furious. In 1799, he secured passage of a law called the Logan Act, which forbade any American citizen from engaging in unauthorized negotiations with a foreign government.

This act was the new American government's first attempt to restrict citizen activity in the formulation of foreign policy. In the Washington administration it had been made clear that citizens did *not* make foreign policy by mob action or by public debate. But by such legislation as the Logan Act, the government of the United Staes, so close to its own revolutionary days, hemmed itself in against unpleasant ideas, and cut off one informal means of arriving at bases for negotiation with foreign governments. This peculiarity of the American official character was to continue: the Logan Act remained on the American law books and was an integral part of American foreign policy in the difficult days of the mid-twentieth century.

(Two other major problems marked the diplomacy of the United States in these days. The first problem was an unofficial war with France. War was not declared between the

United States and France, but, as far as many ships and sailors on the seas were concerned, it might as well have been. Using ruses, and sometimes outright open attacks, warships of both nations attacked each other's ships. The second problem was the troublesome series of incidents that involved the Barbary pirates. Theoretically, the Dey of Algiers and the rulers of Tunis and other cities along the North African coast were subjects of the Sultan of the Ottoman Empire. In fact, they were rather more personal rulers of independent feifdoms, and they increased their fortunes and vented their spleens by capturing the ships and sailors of various European trading nations and of the United States. For many years, various attempts were made; sometimes even bribes and tribute were paid by the American government to avoid troubles. The difficulties ranged for decades, providing one of the bravest eras in the history of the United States Navy, when men like Commodore Preble and Captain Stephen Decatur made names that would go down in history. Unfortunately space does not permit more than a mention of these interesting times.)

Secretary Pickering was a most destructive force in the conduct of American foreign relations. It became apparent to President Adams that Pickering was seeking desperately to foment war with France, and he was finally dismissed in the spring of 1800. He was the only Secretary of State to be actually dismissed from office.

In the spring of 1800, John Marshall was appointed Secretary of State. He came into office at a desperate time. Pickering had allowed affairs with France to become so serious that it seemed only a matter of time before war would be declared between the two countries. A second mission to France was

John Marshall

moving very slowly. Marshall was every bit as much an influence for peace as Pickering had been in influence for war.

Marshall was a man of many talents, largely unrecognized by history save as Chief Justice of the United States Supreme Court. He was a man of strong principle and strict public advocacy of principle. During a term in Congress he had distinguished himself by standing for principle in a difficult case that involved a deserter from the British navy and a mutiny aboard the frigate *HMS Hermione*. President Adams had allowed a district judge to hear the pleas of the deserter and of the British consul when the deserter was found on American soil. It was proved to the judge's satisfaction that the deserter was an Irishman, not an impressed American seaman as he claimed. But had he been an American, Marshall told the House of Representatives, the mutiny the man instigated would not have been mutiny at all but a search for freedom.

Marshall combined his love of freedom with a strong feeling for the need to accept and obey international law as a means of settling disputes among nations.

America was a small nation, weak and undefended, without a standing army and with a very small navy. Diplomatic relations were still conducted with only five countries, and matters had changed little since the days of the Department of Foreign Affairs. Adherence to the principle of international law provided America's greatest possible protection.

When President Thomas Jefferson appointed James Madison as Secretary in 1801, the salary of the Secretary had been raised to $5,000 a year, the chief clerk received $2,000 a year, and a number of new clerks had been added to the department. But the total domestic expenditure for salaries was still less than $13,000. The Department of State was a small department of a very small nation.

James Madison

President Jefferson was a strong-minded man, and he possessed a thorough understanding of foreign realtions. A few weeks after the new administration took office, Jefferson learned that France had made a treaty with Spain which would give France control of the huge Louisiana Territory, an area extending far north and west of the Mississippi River. If France did take this territory, she would remain a constant threat to American independence and expansion.

Jefferson had a problem. The Virginia Republicans were, or tended to be, strict constructionists of the Constitution. The American Constitution, they said, gave certain powers to different branches of government, and the federal government should not have powers not specifically granted to it. For example, the Constitution did not empower anyone to add to the land holdings of the United States.

Despite this, Jefferson decided that he must do everything possible to prevent the French from moving back into North American affairs, now that they were out of Canada. He sent Robert Livingston, former Secretary of Foreign Affairs, to Paris as minister to negotiate with the French for the territory or part of it. He sent a letter to Livingston by the hand of Eleuthère du Pont de Nemours, the gunpowder maker from Delaware. Livingston had a remarkable, almost frightening, offer from the French for *all* of Louisiana, and Jefferson put aside his strict-constructionist scruples and bought the territory.

In Congress, there were some who said the treaty was unconstitutional because it went beyond the powers granted the President or Congress. But the chance to double the territory of America was too great to be passed; and the whole balance of power between the old states, the North and the South, was thus changed.

By and large, Jefferson was his own Secretary of State.

During his administrations, the troubles with Britain became most serious, largely because of impressment of American seamen and the stopping and searching of American ships by the strong British navy. Secretary Madison was influential in several ways. He supported the idea of an embargo on trade with foreign nations in order to keep British ships out of American waters, to keep American ships out of trouble and to hurt the British by cutting off trade.

Had the embargo been levied against Britain alone, it might have hurt British trade. But the embargo was placed against all foreign trade, and American businessmen simply did not honor it. John Jacob Astor sent ships all around the globe. He shipped furs out of Canada to avoid the law. Other merchants shipped other trade goods. The result was that law-abiding Americans were hurt, and the embargo was a failure.

Since President Jefferson was so much his own Secretary of State, Madison could hardly shine as policy maker. Madison was an excellent Secretary in the sense that he worked just as Jefferson wanted him to work.

The next Secretary of State added a new element to the body politic. He was Robert Smith, Secretary of the Navy under President Jefferson. Smith had been a good Navy Secretary. He was helped greatly in his political life by personal relationships—his brother was a United States senator. In this first 25 years of American history, the Virginians dominated the new government, John Adams of Massachusetts being the great exception. Washington had chosen Jefferson to be his Secretary of State, and this post led Jefferson to the vice-presidency and the presidency. The Secretariat of State led James Madison to the presidency to succeed Jefferson. But when Madison came to the presidency, he was not to have the freedom of choice that his predecessors had been given by Congress. He wanted Albert Gallatin to be Secre-

Robert Smith

tary of State, but Gallatin had important enemies in the Senate, and in a compromise Robert Smith was chosen to be Secretary.

Smith was a navy man, brusque and undiplomatic in his approach to public affairs. He insulted the British crown at a time when it was most unwise for little America to twist the lion's tail. Within a few months, President Madison came to believe that he must have a new Secretary of State, as he found himself doing much of the detail work himself rather than allow Secretary Smith to alienate other nations.

In 1811, Madison indirectly indicated that he would like to have James Monroe, another Virginian, take the Secretariat. When he discovered that Monroe was willing, Madison bluntly told Secretary Smith that his usefulness was ended. Madison offered Smith the post of minister to Russia, but Smith was so angry that he refused it and began to conduct a political campaign against Madison's administration. One might say, then, that in 1811 and 1812 the State Department suffered its first kick as a political football.

There was another change in political usage of the office of Secretary of State. James Monroe was really a political opponent of Madison's in a sense that no other Secretary of State had been to his President. Monroe had tried to run against Madison for the presidency, but had realized quickly that he would be overpowered and had withdrawn. He was elected governor of Virginia before he accepted the State Department post.

Secretary Monroe came to office hoping for a free hand from the President in trying to heal the breach with Great Britain. This breach had become increasingly serious since the embargo of Jefferson had been declared and enforced as well as it could be. The fact was that the United States was being used as a pawn in the war between England and France.

James Monroe

Madison nearly achieved a settlement with England in 1809. It failed because of the intransigeance of the British foreign secretary. France offered America freedom from harassment and advantageous trading conditions, and these were accepted in a new agreement with France in 1810, while the British kept in effect the Orders in Council, which made trade between America and Britain almost impossible.

France had seized some American ships in Italy under French laws which disregarded neutrality, and many Americans were nearly as angry with France as with Britain for mistreatment of American ships and seamen. Britain had been asked to repeal its harsh laws governing treatment of neutral ships, and to stop impressing American seamen. In mid-June, 1812, the British did promise to repeal the Orders in Council and a week later the British Parliament did so. As in the days of Benjamin Franklin, the British adopted a conciliatory policy toward the United States when it was too late. America had declared war on Britain.

Had the transatlantic cable existed there would not have been a war. But the cable did not exist, and there was no way for distrustful Americans to know that talk in Britain about repeal of the Orders in Council was sincere. Thus, America and Britain drifted into a war wanted by no one but a handful of militant patriots in the United States. They were men who advocated belligerent action on the part of the United States to increase its international prestige and to expand its frontiers. They were known as the War Hawks.

Thomas Jefferson had once said that the United States would not extend across the entire land between the Atlantic and Pacific Oceans for a hundred years or more. The War Hawks were already eyeing Spanish territory in the South and British territory in the North. Many distinguished men, including Henry Clay and John C. Calhoun, shared their point of view, one that was to be repeated many times in the course of American history. Even part of their name—hawk —would be applied to men of like views a century and a half later.

It is often said that war is the extension of foreign policy. Some cynics have even claimed that war is the *logical* outcome of foreign policy. Yet, in the course of American history whenever war has come, unless the Secretary of State was endowed with exceptional ability for high strategy, the Department of State has often been subordinated to the military departments, even to the point where policy of the future has been under the influence of the military.

In the War of 1812, many people in New England, in particular, detested the war because it wrecked their business —trade with England, her colonies and the rest of the world. The West and the South enjoyed no such trade and hoped for expansion of territory. They welcomed the war.

Secretary of State Monroe supported the war. He played a unique role, too, for a Secretary of State. For the first and only time in American history, the United States was invaded by an enemy nation and the national capital at Washington was partly destroyed. Secretary Monroe learned of the coming of the British in the second week of August, 1814, and went out to see for himself how close they were. On August 14, he sighted them and sent a messenger to Washington to be sure that the department's records were moved to a safe place. The Declaration of Independence, the Bill of Rights, the secret journals of the Continental Congress, and all the laws, treaties and correspondence of the Department of State were packed into linen bags and taken by cart across the Potomac River to an abandoned grist mill near Georgetown. Later these documents were moved to a house in Leesburg, Virginia, for safe-keeping, and were thus preserved, although many lawbooks and other papers were burned by the British in their assault on the Capitol and the other government buildings.

The War of 1812 lasted for nearly three years. After the burning of Washington, Secretary of War John Armstrong was in disgrace, and his job was taken over by Secretary of State Monroe. On the advice of Secretary Monroe, the President appointed a commission of five men to conduct peace negotiations. The commission included Henry Clay, a hawk, and John Quincy Adams, basically a dove, to use a twentieth-century term. The commission was extremely skillful, and, in the peace negotiations that led to the Treaty of Ghent, the Americans managed to eliminate all the troublesome problems of restrictions and border disputes between the United States and Britain which had hung over since the unsatisfactory end of the Revolutionary War. The Secretary of State was not present at these negotiations in Europe, but his instructions were given in writing to the negotiators.

In 1816, James Monroe succeeded James Madison as President, thus bringing about charges that the Virginians were establishing a dynasty in the United States. As the record shows, it cannot be simply said that the stepping stone to the presidency was the State Department post. (It certainly led Robert Smith nowhere.) But Jefferson, Madison, and Monroe had all served as Secretary of State, and all succeeded eventually to the presidency. So the talk persisted.

President Monroe chose John Quincy Adams of Massachusetts as his Secretary of State. One reason for this was to quiet the talk about a Virginia dynasty. President Monroe was conscious of the need for a New Englander in high position in his administration if he was to succeed as a political leader of the American people.

Such political considerations do not always bring the best

John Quincy Adams

man to the job, as in the case of Robert Smith, who was well suited to direct the nation's naval affairs but totally unsuited for the delicate tasks of diplomacy. Yet in selecting John Quincy Adams, President Monroe chose the one man in the United States who was better suited than any other to direct American foreign relations.

As a child, Adams had accompanied his father, John Adams, to Paris when Adams was sent as a commissioner of the Continental Congress, and he had helped his father with secretarial work. When he was only 14, young Adams had served as secretary to Francis Dana, the American minister to Russia. In 1783, he had been a secretary to the American delegation that negotiated the end of the Revolutionary War with the British. In 1794, when he was only 27 years old, John Quincy Adams had been appointed minister to the Netherlands, where he had served until he was transferred to Berlin. In 1801, Adams returned to the United States, where he served as Massachusetts state legislator and learned the ways of politics (which he grew to hate). In the spring of 1803, he was chosen by the legislature to represent Massachusetts in the United States Senate. Here he proved himself so independent that he aroused the enmity of Massachusetts political leaders. After he deserted the Federalists of Boston to support President Jefferson's embargo against foreign shipping, he was defeated in his bid to return to the United States Senate, and it seemed that his political career was at an end. But he went to Russia as minister and acquitted himself very well, and even more worthily at the negotiations for the Treaty of Ghent. He was rewarded by appointment as minister to Great Britain, where he proved himself a steadying force in the difficult interplay between mother country and former colony.

John Quincy Adams probably possessed fewer illusions

about his own character than any political leader of his time: "I am a man of reserved, cold, austere, and forbidding manners; my political adversaries say, a gloomy misanthropist, and my personal enemies, an unsocial savage. With a knowledge of the actual defect in my character I have not the pliability to reform it."

Yet, as Secretary of State, Adams was to be immensely successful, because he possessed the intelligence, the knowledge, and the courage to work out a practical foreign policy for America and the ability and determination to carry out the details. President Monroe's greatness lay very much in his ability to make best use of this turbulent but brilliant servant of America.

President Monroe and Secretary of State Adams made a remarkably effective team in the conduct of American foreign relations. Adams was a workhorse. He was bright and sharp and an excellent organizer of the details of the State Department. When he arrived in Washington, he learned that routing and filing of documents were so carelessly handled that a treaty had been lost. No one knew how many important letters and documents from statesmen abroad had remained unread or could no longer be found for reference. Adams changed this by establishing a tight system in the State Department. Although he detested the routine tasks of the State Department, yet Adams was so conscientious that he devoted his Sundays to answering correspondence and preparing instructions for ministers who would be sent abroad. Soon, although the United States spent less on management of foreign affairs than the British spent on espionage for the foreign office, the American foreign service began to take on a professional status.

By 1818, the organization of the Department of State was fairly well completed. Under the Secretary was the chief clerk, and under him worked other clerks, each in charge of some special section of the department's business. One kept track of the correspondence with the foreign consulates regarding trade. One copied letters, made out passports and cipher letters for the department, and filled out various papers for the Secretary's signature. Another prepared the acts of Congress for publication and handled claims against foreign governments. If the problems became knotty, the Secretary was called in to resolve them. Altogether there were about a dozen persons in the State Department at this time, and among their numerous duties was the conduct of the census of 1820, for which the Secretary of State was made responsible by Congress.

The fact that under Secretary Adams the State Department became more efficient than it had ever been was not Adams' most important contribution. For several years, there had been frictions among the Americans in the South, the Seminoles and other Florida Indian tribes, and the Spanish who controlled the territory. General Andrew Jackson invaded Spanish territory in 1818, and although many congressmen disapproved of the action, Secretary Adams approved, and supported Jackson within the cabinet when the matter was discussed. Adams also took a strong line with the Spanish government and eventually secured for the United States possession of East Florida, which gave the United States the whole peninsula. Adams traded $5,000,-000, and whatever title the United States had, to claim the territory called Texas.

The most significant international matter during Adams' years as Secretary of State concerned the Spanish colonies of the South American continent and Central America. Early in the nineteenth century, the seeds of revolutionary activity began. By 1816, Simón Bolívar had formed a Republic of La

Plata in the south, and there was a call by some Americans that it be recognized and that Spanish sovereignty over all Latin America be disavowed.

In the summer of 1816, Secretary Adams was asked to prepare a statement of position for the United States.

> I am satisfied [he wrote President Monroe] that the cause of the South Americans, so far as it consists in the assertion of independence against Spain is just. But the justice of a cause, however it may enlist individual feelings in its favor, is not sufficient to justify third parties in siding with it. The fact and the right combined can alone authorize a neutral to acknowledge a new and disputed sovereignty.

At the end of 1818, the Republic of La Plata seemed to have won its independence from Spain. Simón Bolívar had defeated the Spanish in a series of battles. But the United States was cautious, and it was not until the spring of 1822 that recognition was approved by Congress and funds to support a diplomatic mission were provided.

The defeat of Spain in the New World posed some serious problems for the United States. Until that time the American government's foreign policies had been guided by thoughts of peace and war and expansion of the United States territory on the North American continent.

Gradually, with the realization that Spain was not able to maintain her colonies in Latin America, other countries became interested in the territory. The actions of the Holy Alliance of European rulers, which did not include England, gave some indication that a concerted effort might be made to move in on South America. Perhaps it would result in the acquisition of new colonies by other European powers.

In the summer of 1823, Britain and the United States were both concerned about the trend of these events relative to

Latin America. There was some discussion of joint action with Britain to prevent the destruction of the new independent nations.

President Monroe consulted the two living ex-Presidents, Jefferson and Madison. Both men agreed that the United States ought to act to preserve the freedom of the South American nations. Since Britain was also concerned with freedom of trade in Latin America, it thought the United States ought to join Britain in making it known that an attack upon the former Spanish colonies would be regarded as an attack on the United States.

John Quincy Adams agreed with this principle, but he disagreed that the United States should act in concert with Britain. Russia, for example, had already refused to recognize the new South American governments, which left the way open for her to attack them if she chose to try to restore Spanish rule. Adams did not want to wait for the British; he wanted to act. "It would be more candid, as well as more dignified, to avow our principles explicitly to Russia and France than to come in as a cock boat in the wake of the British man-of-war," he said. Monroe agreed to this idea.

There is argument about who bore more responsibility— President Monroe or Secretary Adams—in formulating the new policy concerning Latin America. Many people were consulted; President Monroe habitually consulted all his cabinet ministers on important matters of state. Some say that Adams played the most vital role. Perhaps he did. Yet as with any vital policy decisions (with some exceptions, such as the Marshall Plan), the policy is usually named for the President in whose administration it was developed.

And so the policy was known as the Monroe Doctrine. It was announced by President Monroe in his annual message to Congress in December. Several historians have credited the part of this message that dealt with foreign affairs to

Monroe himself, and it is apparent that he was the guiding force.

In summary, the doctrine declared that (1) the two American continents (and by extension Central America) could not be subjected to future colonization by any European powers; (2) the political system of the Americas (republics) was essentially different from that of Europe and any attempt to extend the European systems to America would be regarded as dangerous to the peace and safety of the United States; (3) the United States would not interfere with existing colonies of the European nations in the New World; (4) the United States would not take part in European wars. In later years, the entire Monroe Doctrine would be expanded and contracted, and that last part of the declaration would have to be modified.

Times change. Doctrines change. But the Monroe Doctrine was to live a long and useful life. Most important, for the years in which it was developed and announced, it represented America's coming of age in international politics. Until the 1820's, the emphasis of American administrations had been on the most narrow concept of American affairs. This attitude was quite a natural one; the Revolution had to be consolidated and the revolutionaries had to learn to get along among themselves, creating a nation from the raw materials offered by colonies and territories, including even the independent Republic of Vermont, which had to be assimilated. The process took nearly half a century, slowed as it was by an unhappy second war that drained the infant republic of much of her growing strength.

But by 1823, the United States of America was no longer infant or adolescent. With the enunciation of the Monroe Doctrine, the administration showed that the nation was ready to accept the responsibilities of nationhood in a hard world.

Politics and High Office

The first four Presidents of the United States chose their Secretaries of State on the basis of personal loyalty or personal ability without consideration for the political importance of the post. Yet, during those first administrations, it was becoming clear that the office of Secretary of State afforded a convenient jumping-off point for a politican who sought the presidency. It was more than coincidence that Thomas Jefferson, James Madison, James Monroe, and John Quincy Adams all served as Secretary of State and then were elected to the presidency.

It was true that John Adams had been the first Vice-President of the United States and second President, and that Thomas Jefferson had served under Adams as Vice-President before being elected third President of the United States. Until 1801, the vice-presidency had been most important in the line of political succession. But then Aaron Burr was elected Vice-President, followed by George Clinton who served two terms, Elbridge Gerry, and Daniel D. Tompkins, and for all these men the vice-presidency was the end of the line. By 1824, it appeared that the State Department was a more likely post for an ambitious man than the vice-presidency.

A background in politics seemed important too. A man who was to be President ought to have achieved a certain recognition among his constituents. For example, James Madison served in Congress, James Monroe was for a time United States senator from Virginia, Thomas Jefferson had been a member of the Continental Congress, John Quincy Adams had been a senator, and, of course his father, John Adams, had been Continental Congress delegate.

Having achieved so much recognition, and carrying the backing of their people at home, these men had then risen to national or federal importance through their accomplishments in the field of diplomacy. A man who was striving for power would seem to find a pattern in the lives of the former Presidents, and so the State Department post had become elevated in popular importance.

President Monroe's administration was characterized by a seeming political calm in the United States, known as the Era of Good Feeling, but this calm did not prevent a number of men from beginning to seek the presidency almost from the day that Monroe was inaugurated for his second term in office.

The United States, in 1824, was embarrassed by a surplus of brilliant and talented men seeking an office that only one of them could occupy. The Virginia dynasty had run its course, and although two Virginians served in Monroe's cabinet, neither was seriously considered for the presidency, nor was any member of Congress from that state a real candidate. For one thing, Virginia was no longer the most populous state. New York had passed it. So early in the 1820's, the men under consideration for the nation's highest office were William Crawford of Georgia, Secretary of the Treasury; John C. Calhoun of South Carolina, Secretary of War; Henry Clay of Kentucky, Speaker of the House of Representatives; Andrew Jackson, a general in the American army; and John Quincy Adams.

Crawford was the favorite of the Deep South, Clay was the candidate of the West and Middle States. Calhoun, also a Southerner, was persuaded to withdraw because of his youth and seek the vice-presidency. Andrew Jackson drew his support from Clay, Calhoun, and Crawford territory.

In this period of American history, different states followed different customs in the election of Presidents, but the electoral college was a far more important body then than it was to be in the twentieth century. So were the various legislatures. One example of the system was New York, whose electoral votes were to precipitate a crisis in the elections in 1824.

Under New York's election law, the state's two legislative houses voted separately on candidates for the electoral college. Each set of candidates was pledged to support a particular man for President (and another for Vice-President). If the two houses could agree on the same candidates, all was well. If they disagreed, then a joint session was called and the committee of the whole legislature decided on one set. These men then went to Washington to vote in the meeting of the electoral college, pledged to support the candidates for the presidency in whose names they had been selected.

In the New York election of 1824, the two houses disagreed, which was quite understandable with so many presidential candidates in the field. In the joint meeting that followed, the legislators agreed to send 26 representatives to the electoral college to vote for John Quincy Adams. Of the total of 36 votes to be cast, Clay was second in the running.

Since four strong men were running for President in 1824, it was most unlikely that any one of them would receive an absolute majority of the votes cast in the national electoral college; so no one was very much surprised when the college was unable to select a President. The names of the three candidates who had polled the greatest number of votes were placed before the House of Representatives, which was to select the next President.

Andrew Jackson had emerged as the strongest candidate, with 99 electoral votes. John Quincy Adams had won 84 electoral votes, including the solid vote of New England and most of the New York votes. William Crawford had polled 41 votes, mostly from Virginia and Georgia. Henry Clay had polled 37 votes, so he was out of the running.

Yet Clay was in the position of being the man of the hour, the man who could sway the elction. Crawford might do the same, but Crawford would not give up hope that he could split the other votes, so the key lay in the Clay votes.

In the weeks between the unsuccessful meeting of the electoral college and the convening of Congress, all three candidates for the Presidency sought Henry Clay's support. Each man would have made Henry Clay Secretary of State had he asked. Clay wanted the post; he had wanted it for several years and had been much chagrined in 1817 when President Monroe chose instead John Quincy Adams.

Henry Clay had quarreled with Adams a number of times, but he also had quarreled with Andrew Jackson. Clay did not give serious consideration to throwing his support to Crawford, because Crawford had suffered a stroke before the election and Clay did not approve of voting for a sick man.

Jackson dined with Clay several times. Adams paid a courtesy call on Clay and his friend Congressmen Robert

Letcher. In these meetings, both Jackson and Adams indicated their friendliness to Clay.

The decision as to who would be the sixth President of the United States, then, lay in the hands of Henry Clay. Was it any wonder that no matter what he decided he would be maligned in the future by the friends of the man he did not choose? Clay was approached by James Buchanan in behalf of Jackson, but Clay decided to work for Adams' election, and he asked his supporters to throw their votes to the Massachusetts man. He did not control the election; it was not that simple. Jackson controlled the votes of 11 states in the House of Representatives. Adams controlled seven states and needed six more. Missouri and Illinois, which had voted for Jackson originally, were persuaded (one congressman from each) to vote for Adams. Maryland, another undecided state, was persuaded to vote for Adams. And then Clay threw his three states to Adams, and John Quincy Adams was elected by a majority of one state on the first ballot.

No one had seriously tried to interfere with the selection of cabinet officers in the past, but in 1825 John C. Calhoun, the newly elected Vice-President, told President Adams that if he appointed Henry Clay Secretary of State he would lose the support of the South and West. Possibly, Calhoun's statement forced Adams to a decision, because, given Adams' character, such a threat would be sure to cause him to do exactly what he was warned against doing. Perhaps there were political considerations. In any event, Adams did make Clay Secretary of State.

Then the furor began. The supporters of Andrew Jackson, in particular, claimed that Adams had made a political deal with Clay before the election in the House of Representatives. This charge was never proved, and Adams later denied it:

Henry Clay

As to my motive for tendering him the Department of State when I did, let that man who questions it come forward. Let him look around among statesmen and legislators of this nation and of that day. Let him then select and name the man whom, by his preeminent talents, by his splendid services, by his ardent patriotism, by his all-embracing spirit . . . by his long experience in the affairs of the Union, foreign and domestic, a President of the United States, intent only upon the welfare and honor of his country, ought to have preferred to Henry Clay.

Adams' and Clay's intents are still matters for speculation by historians, but the course of events after the fateful appointment is a matter of record. In his history of the Department of State, Stuart says that the appointment of Clay was Adams' most serious mistake as President. Morison, in his *Oxford History of the American People*, says that Adams' most serious mistake was to stand strong for nationalism at a time when states' rights advocates were growing strong. Other historians have other judgments on the John Quincy Adams administration, but generally it was considered a failure as far as administration went, the first such failure in the history of the nation.

Studying the administration from the standpoint of the Secretary of State and American foreign policy, the question of failure does arise, but it was not failure of this brilliant administration so much as failure of Congress to understand the needs of the nation. If John F. Kennedy could be cited favorably more than a century later for vision and brilliance in policy, so could John Quincy Adams. The two shared one problem: the intransigeance of a Congress that would not do what they wanted.

From another viewpoint, the Adams administration

marked a change in America and the position of the Secretary of State. For the first time a cabinet officer was openly reviled and held responsible for actions for which the President should have been held responsible. This forcing of the Secretary of State, an administrative official, into the political arena was to become a recurring theme in American political life. Never would it be more hostile, more open, and more irresponsible than it was in the John Quincy Adams administration when Henry Clay was Secretary of State. Not even Dean Acheson, maligned so seriously during the McCarthy era, would be so threatened, politically and personally, as was Henry Clay.

Senator John Randolph of Roanoke, Virginia, arose on the floor of the United States Senate and flatly accused President Adams and Clay of making a political deal. He referred to these men as "the combination unheard of till then, of the Puritan with the blackleg." The term "blackleg" was a particularly onerous insult in those days. In its most narrow sense it referred to a gambler who cheated at cards, but more broadly it meant simply "crook."

President Adams might have been annoyed and distressed because he, called the Puritan, was accused of allying himself in a political deal with another man to his own benefit. Secretary Clay could not help but be outraged, for he was accused of political chicanery, and, worse, his personal character was maligned. Clay had a reputation as a hard-drinking man who liked to play cards—a reputation that stood him in good stead in the western state of Kentucky, which was his political stronghold. He could not bear the charge that he was dishonest, however, and he challenged Randolph to a duel.

Dueling was still a custom in America in the 1820's, although it had begun to disappear after the unfortunate affair between Alexander Hamilton and Aaron Burr, which caused Hamilton's death and Burr's disgrace.

Clay and Randolph fought with pistols, neither shooting accurately. Honor was satisfied, but damage was done; and during the four years of the Adams administration, Henry Clay was under a cloud that made his conduct of the office of Secretary of State less effective than it might have been.

Clay was an excellent Secretary of State in the matter of broad policy decision. He was less effective as an administrator because he detested the routine of clerical work; and no matter what else might be said about the State Department, much of its work was always routine and clerical. It seemed that all the dull jobs of the administration were thrown into the hands of the State Department. The Patent Office, for example, was under the charge of the Secretary of State. During Clay's tenure as Secretary, he was fortunate to have a superintendent of patents Dr. William Thorton, who was most efficient in his job. Still, the work was controlled by the Secretary, and he was subjected to a constant stream of letters from inventors and others complaining about the Patent Office.

The Secretary of State was also responsible for copyrights of maps, books, charts, as well as census taking, although Clay did not have a census year with which to contend. The office of the Attorney General of the United States was located in the State Department, and the federal marshals and attorneys took their orders from the Secretary. Actually, not until the creation of the Department of Justice, in 1870, did marshals and attorneys stop reporting to the Secretary of State; and it was not until 1893 that the job of granting pardons to convicted criminals was moved from the State Department.

The Secretary of State was also responsible for supervision of territorial affairs, which became a serious task after the

Louisiana Purchase. More akin to what one would expect of the Department of Foreign Affairs was the job of keeping government and citizens informed about foreign events and trends. Consular officials would prepare such volumes as one on taxation in Europe, a special report on cattle and dairy farming in the world, and consular bulletins on other subjects of interest to foreign traders and, sometimes, American farmers.

Henry Clay did enjoy one great advantage as Secretary. Since he had served twice as Speaker of the House, he had built up a considerable volume of congressional courtesy; that is, he had done favors for people which put them under obligation to him. This situation became valuable when Clay assumed office as Secretary of State, for he discovered that the Department was inadequate to its task.

In January, 1820, the offices of the Department of State had been moved to the corner of Fifteenth Street and Pennsylvania Avenue (where the north wing of the Treasury would later stand). The office space was not a problem, but the management of the office was becoming more complex. In 1820, the United States sent 14 ministers to various countries, plus 110 consuls, four special consuls to the Barbary powers in the Mediterranean, and two agents of claims to Paris and London. In return between 10 and 14 ministers of foreign countries were resident in the United States at all times, plus dozens of consular officers in various cities.

Clay called on the chairman of the House of Representatives Ways and Means Committee, Louis McLane, for help in enlarging his department. On January 14, 1826, he wrote to him, outlining his difficulties and asking for assistance. With the success of the revolutions against Spain, he noted, it had become necessary to send seven ministers to the new powers in Latin America.

Secretary Clay followed this letter with another to Chairman Daniel Webster of a special House committee that was investigating the need for expansion of the executive branch of government. He also suggested the need for relieving the State Department of nearly half of its 15 different classes of duties.

In other words, Clay was the first Secretary of State to suggest that his office be freed of duties other than those pertaining to foreign relations; the duties he wanted eliminated were the domestic responsibilities thrust upon the department in the early days of American government. Clay did not immediately achieve his aim, but eventually the responsibilities for patents, copyrights, the census, and other domestic affairs were removed from the State Department.

Clay's years as Secretary, the years 1825–1829, were remarkable in American foreign relations in one way: They presented a great opportunity to cement friendship between the United States and the new nations of Latin America.

While the revolutionaries of the young United States had been consolidating their gains, the people of Latin America had been struggling for freedom. The announcement of the Monroe Doctrine had aroused hopes in Latin American countries that the United States could be counted on to help in development of a new nation in the South that would not be unlike the American nation in the North. One of the chief revolutionaries, Simón Bolívar, had hopes for a great South and Central American confederation.

In 1825, Bolívar called a conference at Panama to try to iron out regional differences and bring about his dream. The United States was asked to send delegates. This invitation was a challenge to American foreign policy. President Adams was conservative, following the leads of his father and George Washington. He wanted to send delegates, but he

79

wanted them to remain neutral. The President did not want the United States to become involved in any entanglements with foreign countries, especially with Spain.

Henry Clay wanted to turn the Monroe Doctrine into an alliance among all the states of the Western Hemisphere, and, had he been successful in his proposal, many years of unfortunate relations between North and South America might have been avoided.

Clay and Adams agreed on the names of two commissioners to the Panama Conference, and they sent those names to Congress. But when the names were sent to the Senate for confirmation, John C. Calhoun, the Vice-President of the United States, decided that a long, slow look should be taken at the whole idea of sending delegates to the conference. For six weeks, the qualifications of the commissioners were debated, and finally they were approved by a narrow margin. Then money appropriations had to be voted for the trip, and the House of Representatives had its chance to consider the policy-in-the-making. The House considered carefully, and finally passed the appropriation.

By then much time had passed, but the American opportunity was not yet lost. It *was* lost when one of the American commissioners refused to travel to Panama because it was summer and yellow fever and malaria plagued the land. The second delegate did arrive, very late and without his instructions. (During the interminable congressional debates the commissioner had been dispatched unofficially, ahead of the instructions.) A messenger carrying instructions from Clay and Adams was shipwrecked, and the instructions never arrived.

When the Latin Americans met at Panama, they were annoyed by the reluctance of the *norteamericanos* to send official delegates, but they were also willing to forgive. They conducted some business, then adjourned until fall to meet in the healthier climate of Mexico, with the hope that the Americans would come.

Adams and Clay now felt so strongly about the need for cementing inter-American relationships that they asked former President Monroe to attend the conference. Here was opportunity indeed: The man whose name was identified with the most advanced policy in the world to attend the conference! But James Monroe refused, because he did not believe in the cause. And without strong American interest, the opportunity was lost. Britain let it be known that she would block any attempt to achieve hemispheric unity in behalf of her own colonial and business interests. Simón Bolívar became discouraged, and the Mexico meeting never materialized.

The United States would not have such an opportunity in Latin America again for a full century.

The Expansionist Years

The election of Andrew Jackson to the presidency, in 1828, marked the beginning of the Era of Expansion. Jackson brought to the presidency some definite and advanced ideas about the place of the American nation on the North American continent. For the next 32 years, continental expansion continued to be the most important part of United States foreign policy, as well as one of the most important aspects of domestic policy. Jackson appointed Martin Van Buren, one of his presidential campaign managers, as Secretary of State. Van Buren had a great deal of experience as a politican, as a United States senator from New York and as governor of that state, but none as a statesman.

Andrew Jackson was land minded, not sea minded, and he and Van Buren were definitely expansionists, with their eyes on territory Britain also wanted. Consequently, Sir Charles Vaughan, the British ambassador to Washington in this period, wrote home to his foreign office that the administration of the United States was "not disposed to assume the high

Martin Van Buren

tone in their relations with the states of Spanish America which had been assumed by President Adams and Mr. Clay." That statement was mild, compared to the facts. Andrew Jackson remained neutral in the Texas revolution, when the American citizens of that Mexican province rebelled against the central government. The United States sent a sloop of war to the sealing station at the Falkland Islands, and there supported a British claim to that territory, and rounded up Argentine *gauchos* and took them a thousand miles away from home, earning the enmity of the Argentine government that was to persist for more than a century.

As indicated above, the Jackson administration was marked by one very important development in American foreign relations: the resumption of friendly relationships with Great Britain. Henry Clay negotiated a dozen treaties, most of them commercial agreements, with various nations, but it was Jackson and Van Buren who restored truly cordial feelings between the United States and Britain. These relations would have their ups and downs but never again would the United States and Britain break off with one another.

Van Buren resigned as Secretary of State in the spring of 1831, largely as result of an intra-cabinet struggle in which he sided with the President. He was replaced by Edward Livingston, a northern-educated man who had moved to Louisiana and had gone into public life from that state. Livingston's term was not marked by any particular problem or brilliance of action. He did not remain in office long and was succeeded by Louis McLane, who had by now served in the Senate, as minister to Great Britain, and as Secretary of the Treasury. McLane's important contribution to the office of Secretary of State is that he carried out the first important reorganization of the department. It came in 1833, a reflection of the growing power of the United States and the grow-

Edward Livingston

ing importance of foreign policy management in American affairs.

Under the McLane reorganization, the future shape of the department was in part made and in part suggested. The chief clerk of the department became in fact an undersecretary, or administrative assistant to the Secretary, although in name he was still chief clerk. McLane sought an increase in the chief clerk's salary to reflect the growing importance of the job; but Congress ignored the request, and the second most important man in the department continued to receive $2,000 a year.

After 1833, although the State Department continued to exercise domestic functions, the most important division was the Diplomatic Bureau, which had three clerks of its own: one responsible for the missions in England, France, Russia, and the Netherlands; one responsible for other missions in Europe, Africa, and Asia; and one responsible for missions in North and South America. A bureau was established along similar lines to handle consular affairs, also with three clerks, and a Home Bureau with two clerks took care of all domestic papers that fell under the department. A Bureau of Archives, Laws and Commissions was established to handle the department's files; and a Bureau of Pardons and Remissions and Copyrights and the Care of the Library was established.

What McLane tried to do, and accomplished in a very large part, was to separate the foreign relations functions within the department from the miscellaneous domestic functions, with the hope that soon the latter could be transferred to some other agency. Other new offices were included in this reorganization: the Disbursing and Superintending Bureau and the Translating and Miscellaneous Bureau. Also the Patent Office was moved from direct administration of the Secretary.

Louis McLane had been Secretary just a little over a year

Louis McLane

when he quarreled with the President over the action to be taken by the United States in trying to collect money owed it by France. Secretary McLane wanted to take a hard line, and, when the President refused, McLane resigned. He was succeeded by John Forsyth of Georgia—but actually Martin Van Buren, minister to Britain, exerted a strong influence on American foreign policy during the Jackson administration and prevented any Secretary of State from exercising anything like a lone, brilliant role.

John Forsyth had been a member of Congress and had, in fact, served as chairman of the Committee on Foreign Affairs during the Monroe administration. He had been minister to Spain, governor of Georgia and senator from Georgia; but his most important qualification was his friendship with Martin Van Buren. As administrator, he rearranged the bureaus of the department, giving the Home Bureau responsibility for most of the troublesome miscellaneous duties. As innovator, he offered practically nothing, but he served very well in the role of an efficient assistant. The Jackson administration was a strong personal administration, and Secretary Forsyth, the administrator, illustrated a modern aspect of the role of Secretary of State.

In the Forsyth period, relations between the United States and France became strained. During the Napoleonic Wars, the Little Corsican's navy had taken what it wanted where it found it, and this had led to property and damage claims for $12,000,000 by American citizens against France. Nearly 20 years later, the claims were settled by negotiation; and in April, 1834, the first payment came due. The French Chamber of Deputies refused to make the payment, and when it was not made by the end of the year, President Jackson angrily threatened to seize French property in the United States. In the argument that followed, the American minister

John Forsyth

to France returned home and war was very close. The French navy was ready to move, for the French foreign office feared that war would mean the loss of Guadeloupe and Martinique to the United States.

Jackson told Congress in December, 1834, that the United States ought to insist on prompt execution of the treaty or "take redress into its own hands." French Foreign Minister Serurier charged the American President with complaining of *pretended* nonfulfillment of the treaty by France, with the implication that Jackson was telling untruths. It was up to Secretary Forsyth to object to the use of the word "pretended" and he did. Eventually, the affair was settled by the mediation of the British Foreign Secretary, Lord Palmerston. But during the discussions between nations, Secretary Forsyth made one important declaration that concerned the American method of carrying out foreign policy. In any discussion, he said, the *sincerity* of the opposing party must never be questioned. "Facts may be denied, deductions examined, disapproved and condemned without just cause of offense" but the integrity of the government concerned must not be questioned.

When the treaty matter was finally settled, the French word *"prétendu"* was discovered to mean "alleged" or "socalled," and not "pretended," as it had been mistranslated by Americans. A distinguished Secretary of State might have verified the translation first (although in the case of Andrew Jackson it probably would have made no difference). But such a Secretary of State would not have survived in the Jackson administration, because Jackson was his own Secretary of State. Forsyth's role with Jackson, and with Van Buren after him, was to carry out the foreign policy of the President, not to formulate that policy. Such duties demanded a special type of person, a self-effacing, hard-working man who was willing to be wrong in behalf of his superior's ideas or who considered only the means with which he might carry them out. There were to be a number of such Secretaries of State, but Forsyth was the first of them.

Forsyth's career also illustrates another difficulty in American foreign relations caused by the lumping together of foreign policy management and certain quasi-judicial duties. The affair was the case of the Spanish ship *Amistad*, which wandered into American waters in a peculiar manner.

The *Amistad* was owned by a Spanish captain named Ferrer. In the spring of 1838, Captain Ferrer shipped a cargo of some 40 African slaves from Havana, intending to carry them to another port on the island for use on a Cuban plantation. Out of port, however, the slaves rebelled, killed Captain Ferrer and another member of the crew, imprisoned two Cuban businessmen who were nominally their owners and set about trying to sail the *Amistad* back to Africa.

Since the Africans did not know how to navigate, they boxed the compass for days, and finally ended up on the shore of Long Island not far from Connecticut waters. They were picked up by an American navy brig. The *Amistad* was towed into New London harbor, and the Africans were seized to stand trial.

Immediately a conflict arose about the Secretary of State's various duties. For one thing, Secretary Forsyth was approached by the Spanish minister, who insisted that the *Amistad* came under the terms of the Spanish-American commercial treaty. The ship and its cargo were property, and so were the slaves, he said. All the United States need do was turn over the ship, slaves and cargo to the Spanish government. But Secretary Forsyth was also approached by the United States District Attorney for Connecticut, because under federal law the District Attorney reported to the Secretary of State. The District Attorney said that a preliminary hearing had been held in New London, and that a federal district judge had bound over the *Amistad* captives for trial. The District Attorney wanted to know what he should do.

President Van Buren wanted to restore the *Amistad,* its cargo, and the slaves to the Spanish government, but Secretary Forsyth could not function entirely as advocate because his subordinate had a judicial duty as an officer of the court. So the case dragged on uncomfortably for nearly three years, with John Quincy Adams entering it as advocate for the *Amistad* captives and pleading their case in the United States Supreme Court. In the end, the United States was much embarrassed, and the Department of State was embarrassed in particular when the United States Supreme Court freed the *Amistad* captives as persons illegally enslaved.

Two of Van Buren's policy positions in foreign affairs were instrumental in his defeat for reelection, in 1840, by William Henry Harrison. They were his refusal to play politics with the Canadian problem and his politicking with the issue of slavery. Thus, when Harrison became President in 1841, the formidable Daniel Webster became Secretary of State, a strong man given a strong position at an important time in American history.

Daniel Webster and John Forsyth are examples of two extremes of character and performance in the office of Secretary of State. Where Forsyth was careful and inconspicuous, Webster was dashing and even careless with the responsibilities entrusted to him. Because Webster wanted someone he could trust absolutely in the post of chief clerk, at the very beginning of his office he outraged many members of Congress. He appointed his son Fletcher Webster as chief clerk and then often left Washington on vacation, giving his son more power to negotiate and run the department than any

Daniel Webster

other Secretary had ever given any other clerk.

Like Forsyth, Webster was also involved in a court case, one arising from the difficulties along the Canadian border dating from the previous administration. The Canadians had attacked the American steamer *Caroline*, which was supplying the Canadian rebels; and an American named Durfee had been killed. Later, a Canadian named Alexander McLeod had boasted while drinking that he had killed Durfee. McLeod had been arrested and ordered to stand trial in New York State.

When the news of the arrest reached London, the British government was upset. Britain had already said that the attack on the *Caroline* was an official act of British troops and that if McLeod was tried for murder, British public opinion would be inflamed. Soon public opinion *was* aroused, and so was opinion in northern New York.

Eventually, the McLeod case was tried. McLeod was acquitted of murder, but more important from the standpoint of American foreign policy, a bill was drafted for Congress by Daniel Webster that would give federal courts the power to issue writs of habeas corpus and to place under federal jurisdiction any person accused of a crime committed under the instructions of a foreign country. This bill was passed by Congress in 1842 and became part of the body of American law, a vital protection for the nation against action by individual states which could jeopardize the common safety.

Daniel Webster moved on a large scale and brought a new dimension to American diplomacy, although it was not a dimension always present in future administrations. In a way, Webster was a larger figure in American life than either of the Presidents he served as Secretary of State, Harrison and John Tyler. He had broader tastes, for one thing. The British government sent Lord Ashburton to the United States as a spe-

Abel P. Upshur

cial ambassador, with instructions that he was to try to negotiate settlement of all outstanding difficulties between the two nations. Webster rented a large house on Lafayette Square, near the White House, for the British visitors and arranged a round of parties and entertainments to amuse them. So successful was he with this approach that a friendly and very favorable treaty was secured, the Treaty of Washington, which adjusted boundary differences, and did, indeed, put an end to the various difficulties that remained between the two nations.

Webster quit the Tyler cabinet in disagreement over the expansionist policy. He was not an expansionist. Tyler was committed to the annexation of Texas; and so the pair parted company, though amicably. The next Secretary was Abel P. Upshur, about whom it could best be said that he did as his President told him. As to how he did it, that was another matter. Upshur turned out to be the least capable of the Secretaries of State, totally devoid of tact and so brutally frank in his approaches to diplomacy that his exchanges with the Mexican minister in Washington sounded almost as preludes to declarations of war. Upshur is notable for the manner in which he ended his service. On February 28, 1844, he and President Tyler and other members of the cabinet set out on an excursion aboard the *USS Princeton,* a new auxiliary screw frigate which boasted a pair of 12-inch wrought-iron guns called Oregon and Peacemaker. As the ship moved along the river and the gay party watched, the new guns were fired. Peacemaker exploded, killing Upshur, Navy Secretary Gilmer, one other man, and causing serious injury to 20 other notables aboard.

John C. Calhoun became Secretary of State, chosen by President Tyler to further his own political ends. Calhoun, one of the most important men in the nation, was known to

John Caldwell Calhoun

favor Texas annexation. Although Calhoun completed the negotiations for the annexation, his and Tyler's plan was defeated; the United States Senate refused to ratify the treaty. Calhoun negotiated another treaty of annexation, but it, too, was rejected. Finally, he and Tyler achieved by another means the goal that they could not secure in the usual diplomatic fashion. In 1844, James K. Polk was elected President, having run on a ticket which called for the annexation of Texas. After the election, President Tyler called on Congress to annex the territory by joint resolution rather than by treaty, and Congress did so just before the end of the Tyler administration.

Calhoun was Secretary of State for less than a year, and during that period there was only one real international issue, at least only one to which the American government was willing to address itself, and that was Texas. If Calhoun's diplomatic career seems extremely one-sided and narrow, that is a reflection of the temper of the times; much in the way of foreign relations that should have been looked after in this period was allowed to languish and create newer and larger problems for succeeding administrations.

Calhoun left office with the retiring Tyler administration. President Polk came in with a new Democratic administration, and as his Secretary of State he chose James C. Buchanan, a Pennsylvanian, who was eminently qualified for the job, having been a senator and a minister to Russia.

President Polk attached some conditions to the Buchanan appointment. It had been the practice of various Secretaries of State to attempt to use the office as a stepping stone to the Presidency. John Quincy Adams had done so. Martin Van Buren had done so. Henry Clay and Daniel Webster had certainly done their best to use the position to secure the presidential nomination. Polk was convinced that no man

James Buchanan

should use a high appointive office as a springboard for a higher elective office. So Polk asked Buchanan to promise that he would retire from the cabinet if he decided to become a candidate for the presidency or vice-presidency. (This condition applied to all other cabinet officers, too, but it was specifically directed at Buchanan.)

In the spring of 1845, the United States faced two basic questions of foreign policy. One was brought about by the Tyler administration's action on Texas. The other question, to which little attention had been paid by previous administrations, was the determination of the northwestern boundary between the United States territory and that claimed by Britain in behalf of Canada. The Americans claimed land as far north as the southern point of Russian America (Alaska). The British claimed lands as far south as the Columbia River that runs between Washington and Oregon. During the election campaign of 1844, a popular slogan had been "Fifty-four forty or fight!" This referred to the 54th parallel as the northern point of the American claim. When they came to office, President Polk and Secretary Buchanan recognized the impossibility of pressing so great a claim and were willing to settle for a boundary at the 49th parallel, but in the negotiations British Minister Pakenham upset the apple cart by rejecting this American proposal.

Buchanan's handling of the situation illustrates how foreign policy is sometimes made and shows the value to a President of a level-headed Secretary of State. British Minister Pakenham was contemptuous and insulting in his out-of-hand rejection of the American proposal. President Polk was angered, as were dozens of congressmen, and the American offer was snatched away. Polk was so angry that he refused to continue negotiations with the British, and for a time it seemed that the autumn of 1845 might bring an outbreak of violence along the northwestern border, and even war between the United States and Britain.

But Secretary Buchanan counseled moderation even in the face of British insult. Polk first spoke angrily, but soon he came around to Buchanan's way of thinking. Buchanan said that it was important that the American people and Congress not learn, at that time, of the tone of the Pakenham note. Polk agreed to keep the note secret. Thus, the President had maintained his own position but he had also given his Secretary of State a basis on which to work. Buchanan was not long in taking advantage of this opportunity.

His first move was to write to the American minister in London and ask him to lay before the British foreign office the situation in all its gravity—quite unofficially, of course. His second act was to trace for the British the history of the American claim to 54°40′ as the boundary. British Minister Pakenham soon realized that he had rejected a very generous American offer of settlement, and he asked that it be reoffered. But President Polk was adamant: He would not repeat the rejected offer.

Buchanan was saddled with the task of trying to bring about a settlement over almost insurmountable difficulties. In 1846, the correspondence between Pakenham and the American government was published and public opinion was aroused, making matters worse.

Buchanan's method in these troubled times was to meet frequently, and informally, with Minister Pakenham, discussing the border problem in all its aspects and remaining alert for some sign of an opening for a new *démarche*, as an approach is called in diplomatic language.

In these private discussions, the diplomats were exceedingly and sometimes shockingly frank. Pakenham admitted that were it not for the claims of the Hudson's Bay Company, the British government would not be interested in the territory in northwest Canada. But because the Hudson's Bay Company was chartered by the government and had been given a semiofficial status, the claims of the company became claims of the government. Actually, Minister Pakenham said, if they could bring the problem to arbitration and the whole territory up to 54°40′ were awarded to the United States, while somehow Britain's pride could be maintained, no one in the British government would be at all disturbed.

Of course these statements were not made in public, nor did Secretary Buchanan publicly say what he had admitted in private—that the American people had been stirred up to follow a policy called "Manifest Destiny," which meant nothing more or less than the domination of the entire North American continent, roughly on a line due west from the northeast and southeast borders.

The policy of Manifest Destiny was as strongly supported by the majority of the American people in 1846 as, for example, would be the American policy of containment of world communism a century later. Americans were as willing to fight to gain control of the northwest territory as they would be willing to fight to keep Communists out of control of Asian countries in the 1950's and 1960's. War was very near, and Pakenham said confidentially that he thought the American people wanted war. Buchanan could demur, but he could not really disagree.

Buchanan set out, nonetheless, to settle the Oregon question, as the territorial dispute was called. He wrote the American minister in London, and said the British must now make a proposal. He suggested that *they* bring up the 49th parallel proposal again. The President could lay that proposal before Congress even though he personally could not accept it because of foolish public statements that had been made by both sides in heat. The Secretary also warned of certain pitfalls, especially of a previous British demand for the perpetual right to navigate the Columbia River. The minister to whom Buchanan wrote was none other than Louis McLane, former Secretary of State, and a man well fitted to engage in such delicate negotiations.

This correspondence occurred in the spring of 1846, which gave Secretary Buchanan another cause for worry. If the dispute with Britain continued into summer and autumn, it would most certainly become a campaign issue in the congressional elections of 1846. Once it became an issue in which the parties took sides, it would become that much more difficult to settle. The danger came from Lewis Cass of Michigan, a demagogue who would have liked nothing better than to begin his campaign for the presidential election of 1848 on the Oregon question. In the settlement of the Oregon question, President Polk guided American foreign policy by establishing the framework. The matter would have to be decided by the Senate, he said. But within that framework, the President gave Secretary Buchanan very much of a free hand, because Polk himself was thoroughly occupied, directing the Mexican war.

That war came about because of a mixture of foreign and domestic problems. Indeed, one must say that from the day of the Compromise of 1820 until the beginning of the Civil War, one major issue overshadowed almost all others in every phase of American policy. It was the issue of slavery. The admission of states to the Union hung on whether they came out of slave or free territory. Mexico had allowed Americans to settle in its northeast provinces, and eventually many of those Americans sought annexation to the United States. Thus, the establishment of an independent Texas, and the relationship of Texas, a slave republic, to the United States, was a matter of racial and slavery issues. In fact, when Texas sought annexation in the 1830's and 1840's, slavery was *the* major issue. Nearly everyone wanted to have Texas in the Union except for the slavery issue. But the Northern states did not want to increase Southern slave power, and the Southern states fought fiercely in council to retain the balance of slave and free states in the Congress.

In the future, race and slave policies would have much to do with American foreign policy. Liberia, the West African nation of freed American slaves, was established in the hope that the race issue might be solved by sending freed blacks "home." But having established the land, whose capital, Monrovia, was named after President Monroe, the Americans let it languish. There had also been a long controversy over the recognition of Haiti, the first black republic in the New World, because Southern Americans could not tolerate the idea of the black state, which had been founded in 1804 after a successful revolution of former slaves.

Buchanan continued to deal with the Oregon question until June, when the British presented an offer that could be given to Congress. On June 12, the Senate accepted the British proposal for settlement, thus removing from the North American scene a serious cause of international dispute.

All this while, Secretary Buchanan was also carrying out instructions from the White House concerning the annexation of Texas. As Secretary of State, Buchanan had done his best to avoid the Mexican War, although from the beginning he knew it was nearly impossible to follow the Polk policy and maintain peace. He sent W. S. Parrott as a confidential agent to Mexico to try to arrange a monetary settlement with the Mexican government for the territory taken by the rebels. He sent John Slidell as minister plenipotentiary to accomplish the same tasks. Although both men failed, and several attempts to negotiate peace with Mexico also failed during the heat of conflict, still it was the task of the State Department to seek diplomatic means of achieving the American government's aims, and that search was not abandoned. In the end, the chief clerk of the State Department, Nicholas P. Trist, managed to secure an agreement that terminated the war, which might not have been ended nearly so satisfactorily or so quickly by a purely military settlement.

It is often overlooked that Secretary Buchanan was far ahead of his time in viewing relations with Latin America as a whole. In spite of the war with Mexico over Texas, the United States sought the preservation of an independent Mexico, and in 1845 when British businessmen began to move into Baja California, Buchanan issued a warning against the attempt of any European country to create a new colony on the North American continent. Two years later, when Britain took advantage of America's preoccupation with Mexico to move into Central America, he sent a diplomatic representative to Guatemala and began to try to bring about an independent federation of the states of Central America.

This active policy was brought to an end, however, with the end of the Polk administration and the election of Zachary Taylor. The problem of Latin America was left to General Taylor and to his new Secretary of State, John M. Clayton. In the beginning it seemed that one would have had to search far to find two less promising diplomats than Old Rough and Ready, as General Taylor was called, and Secretary Clayton, who had risen to prominence as a trial lawyer and political boss. Both of them dealt so indelicately and so harshly with the French minister to Washington in a dispute over French properties that they created an international incident and nearly brought about a breach in Franco-American relations. They were practicing what came to be known as "shirt-sleeve diplomacy," a form of action notable for brusqueness, direct-

John M. Clayton

ness, a lack of sympathy for the forms and protocols of diplomacy, and an outright absence of tact.

Yet Old Rough and Ready and his chief foreign policy aide were quick enough to learn from this incident that protocols and forms had their places in diplomacy. The place was (and is) to maintain open doors and lines of communication between nations, even while the rulers might be cutting each others' throats. One never knew (and still does not in the twentieth century) whether this year's ally would be next year's enemy. So while nations grouped themselves into friendly or unfriendly cliques, the diplomats of these same nations did their best to pass along bad news with a smile and a compliment. The smiles and compliments did much to keep national tempers under control and avoid bloodshed.

Clayton learned the forms but it seems that he forgot the importance of the substance of policy, for he led the United States into a most unfortunate agreement, the Clayton-Bulwer Treaty. It was negotiated by Secretary Clayton and Sir Henry Bulwer, the British minister to the United States. Its aims were to settle the question of an interoceanic canal across the American isthmus, and to stop British attempts to encroach on the weak Central American governments. The two men worked secretly and informally to make the language of the treaty so ambiguous that the parliamentary body of each nation might construe the treaty as a victory for its side. For example, the treaty held that neither side would by itself build or control an isthmian canal and it guaranteed the neutrality of such a canal. This action prevented the United States from building a canal alone, an undertaking already proposed by such men as Commodore Vanderbilt, then one of the leading steamship owners in the United States. For this concession the Americans gained what they thought was a pullout of the British in Central America, from such places as the Bay Islands, Greytown, and the Mosquito Coast (now

British Honduras). But the British had no intention of pulling out of existing colonies, and they interpreted the words to mean that they would not undertake any new excursions into the Americas. So the Clayton-Bulwer Treaty almost immediately became a source of inflammation in British-American relations and forever after remained an object lesson in the senselessness of ambiguous language in treaties between nations. It delayed construction of the Panama Canal by 50 years.

When Zachary Taylor died, after little more than two years in office, Clayton resigned. The new President, Millard Fillmore, asked Daniel Webster to become Secretary of the State Department for a second time. Webster's second term as Secretary of State did not enhance his reputation as a statesman, but it did illustrate an aspect of American foreign policy which had begun before Webster's time and was to continue long after it—the occasional asperity and bluntness with which the United States confronted the world. That this bluntness was almost always based on domestic politics was as true in the case of Webster as it had been with Presidents Polk and Taylor, and others before them.

A revolution in the Hapsburg dominions of Europe in the 1840's had aroused considerable sympathy in the United States. The Taylor administration had sent an American diplomat to Hungary to report on the revolutionary government. It was a handsome gesture by one young revolutionary country to another, but the instructions to the envoy fell into the hands of the Hapsburg minister to the United States and that government protested vigorously to the Department of State. The revolutionary Kossuth government was never recognized by the United States and the revolution failed. But instead of ignoring or softpedaling this unfortunate, unsuccessful *démarche* in the encouragement of revolution, Webster chose to be gratuitously insulting to the Austro-

Edward Everett

Hungarian government, referring to the Hapsburg possessions as "a patch on the earth's surface," with the implication that the Hapsburgs and their government were not worth considering. The difficulties engendered by this undiplomatic exchange continued for a long time.

Webster died in the autumn of 1852. During the last few months of the Fillmore administration, Webster's position was filled by Edward Everett of Massachusetts. Everett was a well-rounded man; he had learned European ways at the famous universities of Göttingen, Paris, Cambridge and Oxford, and he later became a professor of Greek literature and editor of the famous *North American Review*. He had been congressman, minister to England and president of Harvard College. It might seem unlikely that in four months a Secretary of State, no matter how talented or thoughtful, would leave much of a mark on American foreign policy, but Everett did.

The future of Cuba was at that time very much in doubt, and various ambitious men of all nationalities, including American, had ventured onto the island to attempt to overthrow the rotting Spanish regime and set up an independent state or one closely allied to the United States. Cuba, the "Pearl of the Antilles," was an immensely valuable property, physically and strategically, and the governments of France and Great Britain proposed that the United States join a three-party pact renouncing any attempts to take over Cuba.

Everett wrote a letter of refusal on behalf of the United States government, pointing out that no government could pledge itself to maintain the status quo forever. It was an effective argument, reminding the Europeans of the Monroe Doctrine, and it settled many questions that still remained in French and English hearts regarding American attitudes.

America was preoccupied with the domestic issue of slavery when Franklin Pierce succeeded Fillmore in the presi-

William Learned Marcy

dency. The new Secretary of State was a man who was less well fitted by training and experience for the office than any other Secretary of State in history. He was William L. Marcy, a politician from New York State, who had served four years as Secretary of War in the Polk cabinet.

Marcy precipitated several international crises, a very serious one in London, when he forbade American diplomats to appear at the various courts in court dress. At this period of history, diplomats wore ornate uniforms. Ambassadors and ministers vied to outdo one another in uniforms with gold braid and splendid facings. Their swords were often inlaid with precious stones, and some of them managed to appear in court as resplendent as the kings they waited on. Marcy ordered an end to all this finery for American diplomats and, in so doing, made it impossible for a time for Minister James Buchanan to be received at the court of Queen Victoria. The British foreign office took it as an insult to the throne for an American minister to come in the simple black dress of an American citizen. This blunt honesty was all very well, but it did not endear the American diplomats to their fellows or the courts to which they were assigned.

During this period also, an attempt was made to buy Cuba from Spain for $120,000,000 and, meeting at Ostend, Belgium, three American ministers issued a manifesto warning Spain either to sell or to be prepared for the United States to try to take Cuba away. This manifesto aroused serious fears on the part of Spain as to the intentions of the United States in regard to the island. Marcy, who had authorized both the meeting of diplomats and the manifesto, was forced to back down.

When James Buchanan became President in 1856, like so many other Presidents who had served as Secretary of State, he decided that he would make and carry out his own foreign policy. To manage this correctly, he needed a man of prestige

112

Lewis Cass

Jeremiah Black

and pliability, and he found him in Lewis Cass of Michigan, no longer the stalwart and belligerent politician, but, at the age of 75, a mellow old man who had served as general, Secretary of War under Jackson, United States senator, and at one time was Democratic nominee for the presidency.

The thunderclouds of civil war were gathering on the horizon even as James Buchanan and Lewis Cass took office, and matters pertaining to foreign relations seemed to be relatively unimportant. Cass was distinguished for a forceful statement he delivered to all American diplomats abroad on the rights and obligations of neutrals under international law. That was his most salient accomplishment. Jeremiah Sullivan Black, who succeeded Cass in office, is so little known even in the records of the State Department that his biography in an official history of the department, compiled in 1901, is confined to a single paragraph.

Black was a lawyer and jurist. Before coming to the new post he had been Attorney General in the cabinet. Buchanan chose him because he trusted Black and wanted to be his own Secretary of State. Black's term of office was distinguished by only one circumstance: he became the first American Secretary of State to have to deal with Americans as foreigners. During the last days of his tenure the State Department was approached by representatives of the South who came as foreign statesmen. One of Secretary Black's last actions was a set of instructions to American diplomats abroad to prevent the recognition of the representatives of the new Confederate States of America. At the end of Buchanan's term, the expansionist years were ended. The sometimes ebullient, sometimes complacent, sometimes arrogant young American republic was fighting for its life.

The State Department in War

When Abraham Lincoln was elected President in 1860 he chose William H. Seward as his Secretary of State because Seward was the strongest figure in the Republican party. Since Lincoln was a minority President—that is to say, he had been elected by fewer than half the voters of America— every gesture that would promote unity was important to him.

Strange as it might seem, Seward and Lincoln were political enemies, and Seward was not chosen on any personal basis whatsoever. Nor did Seward accept the office because he sought personal aggrandizement. As senator from New York at the time of this crisis, his position of power was very strong. He accepted the office in the spirit in which it was offered him, that of national service.

The Lincoln administration took office on March 4, as was the custom in that day, and on April 1 Seward began pressing for a positive attitude regarding the South and its growing attempt to break away from the Union. Seward suggested a bold policy.

Here was the key to the entire Southern rebellion: if the South could achieve recognition and assistance from a number of foreign states, the Union cause would be lost. If, for example, the British could be persuaded to support the South and guarantee Southern independence, then the Union forces could not fight the South without bringing on war with England. Such a two-front war could scarcely be won, and the Southern cause would have carried.

On April 1, 1860, Secretary Seward submitted a letter to the President, suggesting his very strong line of approach in foreign affairs. He wanted to ascertain the positions of France and Spain, Great Britain and Russia—the great powers. He wanted to send American agents into Canada, Mexico and Central America to arouse a continental spirit of independence and forestall any attempts by European nations to take advantage of the American disruption and obviate the Monroe Doctrine.

At the time, Seward already knew of a new revolution in Santo Domingo, in which the Spanish flag had been raised. He knew of the plans of France and Spain to invade Mexico, and he knew that Britain and Russia had been approached to participate.

On plunging into the duties of his office, Seward first set out to purge the American diplomatic service of persons of questionable loyalty. This task took a great deal of time and consideration, but not so much that Seward was unable to concern himself with the conduct of hostilities. He was the strongest advocate in the cabinet of immediate and effective blockade of Southern ports. From his office in the old two-story building, at the corner of Fifteenth Street and Pennsylvania Avenue, he began a housecleaning, appointing his son Frederick Assistant Secretary of State, and relying on Chief Clerk William Hunter to give continuity to the office and instruct the Sewards in the ways of the department.

William Seward

At this time, there was no civil service in America, and it might have been expected that the new Republican administration would oust all the old Democratic employees and bring in new blood. But Seward's reaction was to retain in office all those clerks and officers who declared their loyalty to the Union. He recognized the special nature of the State Department's activities and was slow to bring in Republicans simply because they were Republicans. As time went on and he became familiar with the office, he did make changes more often, but he recognized the need for experience and continuity in the handling of the special questions of relations with other countries.

President Buchanan's inactive policy regarding Southern secession had left the Union with some serious problems in the field of foreign relations. Buchanan had once said that there was no legal power within the American system to prevent the Southern states from withdrawing from the Union and establishing their own government. In 1861, such a statement carried a good deal of weight with foreign countries and served as a basis for the Confederate claim that the Union had no right to try to coerce the South into remaining a part of the United States.

Early in the spring of 1861, President Jefferson Davis of the Confederacy had sent commissioners abroad to negotiate for the recognition of the Confederate States of America. At about this time, the heads of the various European states began conferring among themselves as to the position they would adopt toward events on the North American continent. Seward learned, to his anxiety, that France and England were talking about a common course of action and had invited Russia to join with them. Such a course could be directed in only one way in the national interests of these powers, toward dissolution of the increasingly powerful

American Union which threatened the colonial power of the Europeans.

Seward was further shocked on May 6, 1861, when the British government announced recognition of the Confederacy as a belligerent power—which meant a left-handed recognition of the Confederacy. The British could trade with the Southern ports in spite of the American blockade. British privateers could seek and get letters of marque, which would let them prey on Union shipping without being declared pirates.

One of Secretary Seward's actions early in the war illustrates the value of diplomatic protocol. Britain and France were considering joint action, and their ministers in Washington were working together. Their announced aim was to secure peace on the North American continent, and they were more than willing that the peace should come about between two more or less equal powers on the continent rather than through victory of the United States. One day, the British and French ministers came to call, together, at the State Department and asked to see the Secretary.

Secretary Seward was in his private office. He might have had the two dignitaries ushered in, and then the fat would have been in the fire, because the British and French ministers bore a joint offer to mediate the war. Mediation could only mean recognition of the existence of the Confederate States of America, and thus the end of the Union contention that the Southerners were misguided Americans engaged in insurrection against their own government. If the Secretary gave audience to the two ministers together, he must give serious consideration to their plan; to reject it would create a serious international problem between the United States and the British and French governments.

Secretary Seward ordered a servant to take the two ministers into the assistant secretary's office, which gave them honor, yet did not compromise the Secretary. Then Seward walked into the assistant secretary's office and appeared surprised to see the British and French ministers together.

"No, no, no!" he said. "This will never do. I cannot see you in that way." He meant that to speak to the two men together would be demeaning to both of them, and that each minister was entitled to the full attention of the Secretary of State under diplomatic protocol. So in spite of the hasty protestations of the two dignified ministers that they were acting under the instructions of their governments, Secretary Seward insisted on giving honor to both men, which could only be done separately. He invited the French minister to dine with him that very evening, and he invited the British minister to come into his office, where he could be received with adequate pomp.

And so the British minister went into the Secretary's office with his offer of mediation. Secretary Seward told him it was quite impossible to receive such a proposal. That evening the French minister came to dine and made a similar proposal; the Secretary gave exactly the same reply. The two ministers could only communicate with their governments, and with each other, privately and commiserate on the failure of their plan. The real purpose of their joint visit, to put diplomatic pressure on the United States government, had been frustrated by the use of protocol.

Seward also proved himself an adroit Secretary of State in another delicate matter. In the autumn of 1861, Jefferson Davis sent James M. Mason of Virginia to England and John Slidell of Louisiana to France to secure outright recognition of the Confederacy. One October night, these commissioners ran the Union blockade at Charleston in the steamer *Theodora*, which took them safely to Havana. There they boarded the British mail steamer *Trent,* whose captain had agreed to give them passage to the British colony of St. Thomas. On arrival at St. Thomas they would sail for Europe.

Between Havana and St. Thomas, the *Trent* was stopped by the United States frigate *San Jacinto.* Captain Charles Wilkes of the *San Jacinto* had two choices. He could put a prize crew abroad the British steamer and take her into an American port, charging that he had captured a neutral vessel carrying "contraband of war." Or he could remove the Confederate officials, and let the *Trent* go on her own way. He chose the latter course as the most humane. But humane or not, it was unwise, because the British government regarded the stopping and seizure of passengers as an insult to the British flag. Troops were ordered to Canada and British men-of-war were made ready for sea.

Matters soon became worse. The *San Jacinto* stopped at Fortress Monroe in Louisiana and then went to New York, where orders were received to take the prisoners to Fort Warren in Boston. When the ship reached Boston, Captain Wilkes was lionized; the Secretary of the Navy congratulated him on his conduct, and the House of Representatives voted the captain a gold medal.

For a month, war seemed ominously close. The British press ranted and British public speakers raved over the insult to the Union Jack. The British government was more restrained than the public, however, and during this month much consideration was given to the nature of the demands that would be made on the United States. Meanwhile, Secretary Seward realized that an unpardonable offense had been committed—and that he must somehow secure pardon; war with Britain in these circumstances was unthinkable.

The British government sent two dispatches to Lord Lyons, the British minister in Washington. They arrived within a few days of each other. The first of these contained a threat and a demand. It directed the minister to demand the immediate release of the prisoners. If they were not released within seven days, Lord Lyons was to close the legation, remove the archives, and notify the admiral of the British Atlantic fleet and the governors of the North American and West Indies colonies—and then return home. Obviously, the first dispatch suggested war.

A second dispatch, however, offered Lord Lyons a bit of leeway. It suggested that he refrain from delivering the first dispatch immediately, but inform Secretary Seward of its contents and ascertain what course the American government would pursue.

Lord Lyons took the second course. On December 19, he presented the substance of the British demands in a call on Secretary Seward at the State Department, and four days later he read the stern official dispatch and left a copy of it with the Secretary.

In those four days, Secretary Seward had already decided what he must do: the British would not stand for less than immediate surrender of the Confederate officials, and he believed the British were quite justified in their demand. The seizure of the men from the ship had been an affront to Britain as serious as any search-and-seizure by Britain in the days before the War of 1812.

Seward settled down, then, to write an answer to the British government.

On Christmas Day and the following day, the answer was debated within the Lincoln cabinet. No one much liked Seward's answer, and most of the cabinet members were inclined—even President Lincoln—to unfavorable reaction. But in the end everyone had to admit that war with Britain would ruin any chance of suppressing the rebellion of the

South, would ruin American trade and would bankrupt the nation if not destroy it.

The Secretary of the Treasury, Salmon P. Chase, was particularly distressed by the answer. "It is gall and wormwood to me," he wrote. But even Chase admitted that it was proper and that it was the only course that could be followed.

In the final reply, Secretary Seward indicated that the United States government quite agreed with Britain, that the British position was that of the United States about search-and-seizure, and that the Wilkes action was totally improper and was carried out without the knowledge or consent of the American government.

Neither Seward nor anyone else in America knew it at the time, but the Seward dispatch followed the exact line of reasoning of the British lawyers who had drawn up the complaint and demand. The note was presented to the British government, and a few days later Mason and Slidell were quietly taken from Fort Warren to Provincetown, Massachusetts, where they were delivered to the captain of the British frigate *Rinaldo.* They arrived in England on January 29, 1862, in an atmosphere entirely changed from that of a few weeks earlier. The British people suddenly felt ashamed for having created so great an incident about what seemed so small a problem in light of the Seward dispatch. As a result, Commissioners Mason and Slidell suffered from too much publicity, and their missions to England and France were never successful, a fact that must be at least in some part credited to the brilliant action of Secretary of State Seward.

During the early months of the war, it was apparent that there was much official feeling in France and England in favor of recognition and assistance to the Confederacy (the French minister, for example, had recommended recognition as early as March, 1861). The Secretary learned from the dispatches of American ministers abroad that the danger of foreign intervention was serious, and he decided on a course unique in American history. He sent abroad a number of unofficial envoys to act as spokesmen for Union interests. Archbishop Hughes, the Catholic prelate of New York went to France. Protestant Episcopal Bishop McIlvaine and Thurlow Weed, the Republican editor, went on other missions. (Seward also sent a pair of American bankers to England with $10,000,000 in American bonds to buy up ironclads that were being built for the Confederacy, but fortunately he did not tell the American minister, Charles Francis Adams, of this improper act.)

Seward became unpopular with Congress during 1862, particularly after the congressional elections of that year, in which the administration suffered serious losses because of the public unpopularity of the war. At one point, a caucus of Republican senators asked the President to fire Seward. Seward heard of the move and offered his resignation. So, then, did the Secretary of the Treasury, Chase, who was at the opposite end of the party spectrum. But President Lincoln stepped in and ordered both of them back to work. He was annoyed at the attempt by Congress to interfere with the activities of the executive branch of the government. This was the first such attempt by Congress in the history of the United States, but it was far from being the last.

Secretary Seward was most adroit in his handling of relations with the great powers of Europe under conditions that sometimes seemed almost impossible. In Britain, for example, the shipyards were building warships for the Confederacy. Seward's protests cut down the efficacy of this building program, and reduced the number of successful Confederate raiders to a handful.

Early in the war, Emperor Louis Napoleon of France decided to utilize the American disruption to move into North America. Advantage was taken of the existence of a monarchical party in Mexico to establish an imperial government there and to put the Archduke Maximilian of Austria on the throne of a nation that was little more than a vassal to France. Louis Napoleon seemed to be egging the United States on, almost hopeful that the Lincoln administration would give him cause to enter the American war on the side of the Confederacy. But Seward's statement about the French move in Mexico was a model of discretion. It was not the American disposition or right to interfere in Mexican affairs, he said, but Americans did know that the people of Mexico favored a republican and domestic government rather than foreign monarchy. There, in all good humor, was a statement of the facts as they were to be lived out in the future. The United States refused to recognize the Mexican monarchy, but was in no position to intervene to stop its establishment.

Secretary Seward realized this in 1863, but members of the United States Senate and House of Representatives were not so wise. They introduced resolutions strongly condemning the establishment of the monarchy. One such resolution was tabled in the Senate but was passed by the House, and when the French government learned of it, the French foreign minister asked, directly and bluntly, the American minister to Paris, "Do you mean peace or war?"

Seward then reiterated the Jeffersonian position that the executive branch of the government made foreign policy, not the legislative branch or any other segment of American government or opinion. So the French were appeased, and another threat to widen the civil conflict was averted. Eventually, as predicted, the Mexican monarchy fell, and poor Maximilian, pawn of a French emperor, was executed by the troops of the revolution, even though Seward tried to save him.

Secretary Seward was badly slashed by an assassin on the night of the murder of President Lincoln. Seward was regarded as a prime architect of the Union victory. He survived, although for a year he was forced to wear a mechanical appliance to keep his jaw in place. He returned to office under President Andrew Johnson and supported President Johnson in his attempts to bring about an easy reconstruction of the Southern rebel states. Seward was largely responsible for the withdrawal of French troops from Mexico, paving the way for the return of Republican government. He negotiated the purchase of Alaska from Imperial Russia. He attempted to secure, by treaty, the purchase of St. Thomas from Denmark, but failed to secure this coaling station in the West Indies because of congressional hatred for the Johnson administration. Congress refused to act simply because Johnson wanted the island.

Seward's last few years in office were uneventful compared to the first; he occupied himself with untangling the after-effects of the war, establishing a basis for the claims against Britain for her part in building and supplying Confederate raiders such as the *Alabama.* The struggle between Congress and the President became so serious in the last two years of the Johnson administration that it would have been impossible for any Secretary of State to have made a record of great accomplishment. Seward had already made his record; by his astute diplomacy he had kept foreign nations from intervening in the Civil War and bringing defeat to the hopes of the Union.

The American Doctrine

The period of American foreign policy from the end of the Civil War until the expansionism of the end of the nineteenth century was marked by an attempt to keep foreign elements from establishing colonies in the Western Hemisphere and by stirrings of colonialism within America itself. There was trouble with Cuba and with Spain. There was trouble with England over South and Central America. The problem of the Panama Canal came up again and again, in spite of the Clayton-Bulwer Treaty; and the French tried to build and control the canal.

This portion of American history runs through four presidential administrations, from that of Ulysses S. Grant, which began in the spring of 1869, through the administration of Chester A. Arthur, which ended in the spring of 1885.

In 1870, the State Department was reorganized by Secretary Hamilton Fish. Fish had almost no qualifications to serve as chief administrator of foreign policy, but he did have good qualifications as an administrator of government affairs, having served as governor of New York and representative and senator from that state. Fish's reorganization of the State Department was important for several reasons. Employees thought it was both fortunate and unfortunate that he was a stickler for accuracy and detail. A seven-hour day was imposed, along with other restrictions on clerks and other officers, such as a ban on smoking in public rooms. The department sprawled into 13 bureaus and offices, from diplomatic bureaus, which were charged with correspondence with American diplomats in various countries, to a passport bureau and a special telegraph office.

Two other changes made by Fish were more important. The department was relieved of many of its domestic legal duties by the creation of the Department of Justice, to whom the United States attorneys and marshals would henceforth report. And a merit system of sorts was begun, to control promotions and salary increases, although the Grant administration in general was known for spreading the spoils system, under which appointments were given in return for favors and for political adherence to the men in power.

The spoils system did extend into the State Department, however, and showed there how vile a means this was for selection of public officials. The minister to Belgium, J. Russell Jones, a former operator of a livery stable, was the uncle of one of the President's secretaries. The consul general to Alexandria was the nephew of a congressman. He drank to excess, brawled, and was involved in a shooting. Worst of all, from the standpoint of American prestige, was the case of John Lothrop Motley, a distinguished historian and a close friend of Senator Charles Sumner of Massachusetts, one of the most prominent of the radical Republicans who held control of Congress. Motley was experienced in diplomacy, for he had served as secretary of the American legation in

Hamilton Fish

Russia and later as minister to Austria. He wore a monocle, parted his hair in the middle, and was certain that he knew more about American foreign policy and what it ought to be than any other man alive.

Motley was appointed minister to London, largely to appease Senator Sumner, who had really wanted him appointed Secretary of State. His major task in London was to negotiate the *Alabama* claims. On his first interview with British Foreign Secretary Lord Clarendon, Minister Motley made so many wild statements and so clearly violated his instructions as minister that President Grant said he would recall him. Secretary Fish was a more diplomatic man; he persuaded the President to allow him to let Motley off with a reprimand, so that Senator Sumner would not be antagonized forever, and this course was followed. But the negotiations on the *Alabama* question were moved to Washington, and Motley was simply permitted to remain in London with nothing to do.

Senator Fish was notable for his handling of President Grant when the Chief Executive kept thrusting unwanted cronies onto the State Department for high appointments. Among other difficulties, President Grant decided he would transfer Minister J. Russell Jones, the prominent livery stableman, from Belgium to the even more rarified atmosphere of the Court of All the Russias. When Secretary Fish learned of this indignity, he sent his resignation to the White House. President Grant, a well-meaning man, was sincerely puzzled and distressed and called Fish to come and talk over the problem. As a result of the talk, the President agreed to refrain from sending any more relatives or cronies to the State Department, and Fish agreed to remain in office. If he had done nothing else during his term of office, Fish had at least won a signal victory for good government.

After the quarrel with Grant, Secretary Fish was allowed

William Evarts

to run matters in his own way, and he turned out to have a very effective system. Much of American government languished during the Grant administrations, and in increasing measure as the years wore on; but the State Department had never been stronger and America had not been represented by a more powerful group of diplomats since the earliest days of the Founding Fathers. Names that would go down in history came into the State Department in these years. John W. Foster became minister to Mexico. Caleb Cushing was minister to Madrid. Elihu B. Washburne was minister to France, one of the most effective ministers to France since Benjamin Franklin. Bancroft Davis was minister to Germany.

So Hamilton Fish's eight years as Secretary of State were most successful, particularly for a man who, when appointed in the spring of 1869, said he had no talent for the task.

Beginning in 1877, the Hayes administration was notable for a strong cabinet, but, alas, not for a strong State Department, headed by William M. Evarts. Fortunately, none of the good work of the Grant administration was undone during that four-year period since no crises developed, and foreign affairs were far from the center of the American stage; these were the years in which the ravages of the Civil War were being repaired.

When James A. Garfield came to the presidency in 1881, he appointed James G. Blaine as Secretary of State chiefly because Blaine had thrown 250 delegates to him at the Chicago convention and had thus secured the Garfield nomination. Blaine was a man of much ambition and great pride in accomplishment, and when he accepted the office he decided that he would create a permanent impact as Secretary of State. He chose as his special sphere of operations the Americas, and came forth with a grand plan—to develop such close relationships with all the American nations that

James Gillespie Blaine

the United States would be paramount in inter-American trade, and the nations of the two continents would live as friends and brothers.

Not since the days of Henry Clay had the Latin nations so much hope of progress as they did in the first few months of 1881. Sadly for the development of Latin America, President Garfield died at the hands of an assassin, and the forward-looking Latin American policy was never carried out. In the winter of 1881–1882, Blaine called for a hemispheric meeting. The new President, Chester A. Arthur, endorsed the idea and the invitations were sent out to Latin American nations. But in December, Blaine resigned as Secretary of State, and when Frederick T. Frelinghuysen became Secretary of State a few days later, the invitations were withdrawn, and with them the chance for Pan-Americanism.

Blaine was much concerned about European efforts to achieve new influence in the Western Hemisphere. These were the years in which a French company under Ferdinand de Lesseps was trying to build a canal across Panama. Blaine would have taken a strong line against the French effort, but he was in no position to do so, and Secretary Frelinghuysen and President Arthur were not inclined to worry about the problem. Most of America's attention was turned inward; immigrants were arriving in droves and industry was thriving. The administration created a civil service system which helped greatly in making the State Department "professional" at the lower levels; but other than this change, there was little to be said for American foreign policy or any innovations brought about by American diplomats, save one. Frelinghuysen was the first diplomat to propose the idea of an international mandate for peoples of backward areas. His proposal came at a meeting in 1884 when various powers met to decide what should be done with the Congo. Blaine sug-

Frederick Theodore Frelinghuysen

gested the neutralization of this area. Yet even here, as was so often the case with forward-looking proposals by American diplomats and Secretaries of State, the plan came to little and the Secretary was berated for stepping outside his bailiwick.

The long period from 1868–1884, then, can be put down as the least active in American foreign relations. The nation was too busy licking its wounds following a nearly disastrous internal war.

The Struggle over Imperialism

In 1884, following a succession of relatively weak Presidents, Grover Cleveland, became Chief Executive. He was destined to be one of the strongest Presidents of all times and one who exerted a powerful influence on foreign policy. In a way, Cleveland single-handedly held the American nation back from making several forays into the imperialism that was so commonly embraced in this period by the important Western Powers. Cleveland did not stop the United States from adventures in imperialism, in the final analysis, but he did delay and weaken the imperialist trend in the United States.

Cleveland's first Secretary of State was Thomas F. Bayard, who had served for 16 years in the Senate, representing Delaware.

Cleveland was noted for his position that public office was a public trust, which meant that he favored merit appointments and disliked appointments made for the sake of politics. Yet he recognized the need for political appointments, and used the State Department's diplomatic and consular services to pay political debts. So, when this first Democratic administration since the beginning of the Civil War came into office, there was an almost clean sweep of the diplomatic service on the ministerial level. The United States maintained 35 diplomatic missions abroad, and 34 new officers were appointed. It was a question of spoils, it was said, and yet there was more to it than that. A strong President wished to have men of his own choosing in high office, and when a President considered foreign relations important, it was normal that he would wish to have as his ministers those who could be considered members of his political family. Moreover, in the case of certain offices abroad, such as Paris and London, money was usually a consideration. Wherever there was royalty to be considered, the posts were expensive, and Congress was never noted for lavish endowment of its officers abroad.

As noted previously, when a strong President is in office, the Secretary of State's role is quite different than when a weak President is in office. The case of Thomas Bayard was no exception. Cleveland was his own executive. Bayard suggested and carried out policies, but he was generally quiet in public and allowed the President to speak for the administration, just as the President wished to do.

The United States had not often been in a position where its leaders played politics with foreign relations, but what tradition there was in this regard received a strong impetus during the Cleveland administration. The reason was that in the 49th Congress the Republicans controlled the Senate while the Democrats controlled the House of Representatives. Since Cleveland's was the first Democratic administration in the reconstituted republic, there were new feelings and new rules by which political men lived. In the same

Thomas F. Bayard

atmosphere that persuaded Cleveland to replace nearly all the Republican appointees in the State Department, the Republican leadership of the Senate was unwilling to allow the Democrats the honor of resolving international difficulties. Thus developed a serious case of partisan politics in the matter of foreign policy.

It came about over the northeast fisheries question. Prompted by Bayard, Cleveland suggested a joint commission of British and American representatives to decide the rules governing fishing in the waters off the American and Canadian coasts. The United States Senate refused to consider the idea, and since the Senate would have the veto power over the membership, that seemed to be that. But there was a way out: the President could appoint members of a "mixed commission" without advice and consent of the Senate, and he did so. But then, when the commission had reached an Anglo-American agreement and a treaty had been drawn, the Republicans in the Senate voted against it on party lines, defeating the treaty, ending months of work most unsatisfactorily, and destroying the confidence of other nations in the negotiating powers of the administrative officials of the United States government.

Political partisans cared nothing for the good of the nation, it seemed. Having seriously disturbed Anglo-American relationships in the fisheries matter, Republican leaders set about trying to use Anglophobia (which was very strong among the large Irish population of the cities) to win the election of 1888. Thus came about the Sackville-West affair, which reflected very seriously on the American government's ability to use tact and discretion in difficult moments.

In September, 1888, as the campaign for the presidency reached its height, Sir Lionel Sackville-West, British minister in Washington, received a letter from a man who called himself Charles F. Murchison. Murchison said he was English-born, although he had become a citizen of the United States. He had a soft spot in his heart for England and he wondered how he should vote in the coming election to help out the old country.

Sir Lionel was foolish enough to allow himself to be trapped. He replied to Mr. Murchison that the Democratic party seemed to be very friendly to England and that if Cleveland was re-elected he would probably be conciliatory to England in future relations.

Of course, there was no Mr. Charles F. Murchison. The letter had been concocted by a Republican politician who took the Sackville-West answer to party headquarters (in spite of professions of secrecy) and released it to the *Los Angeles Times*, a Republican newspaper.

The Republicans immediately began calling Cleveland the "British candidate," and making much of British support of the administration. Neither Cleveland nor Bayard wanted to do anything about it, but Republican pressure was such that the furor would not die down. Sir Lionel made serious errors, giving interviews to the press defending his action and impugning the tricky American politicians.

Finally, the pressure grew so great that Bayard cabled the British foreign office, asking that Sackville-West be recalled. A great British foreign minister would have rescued all concerned by immediate recall, but the incumbent, Lord Salisbury, was a stickler for protocol, and thought he must first have an investigation of the affair.

In a political campaign, there is no time for delay, and Cleveland, after consulting his experts, told the British foreign office that Sackville-West must go, and immediately. The British foreign office took the position that the United States was acting precipitously, and Anglo-American relations were again disturbed.

Relations with Germany took a most unpleasant turn in this period, too, over the question of imperialist expansion of both nations. Germany had begun a serious drive for foreign colonies in 1882 with the formation of the German Colonization Society. One area of German expansion was the Samoan archipelago in the Pacific Ocean. The United States had made a treaty with the Samoan kingdom in 1878 securing commercial rights and the right to establish a naval base at Pago Pago.

The Germans were far more active as traders and colonists than the Americans or the British, who maintained small outposts there. Beginning in 1884, the Germans under Prince Bismarck's vigorous foreign policy began to establish what amounted to an involuntary protectorate over Samoa, and United States citizens began to object. Prince Bismarck discovered that his colonial policies were creating difficulties between Germany and other countries, considerably in excess of the value of the colonies, but in 1888 when the Samoan affair became serious, Bismarck's star was setting. Kaiser Wilhelm II had come to the throne, a young man with strong ideas of his own, and he did not care much for Bismarck or his policies. He wanted a strong navy, strong German colonial position, and action to prove that he had both.

A revolution occurred in Samoa, and the German government declared war against the revolutionaries, then sent German naval vessels to enforce her policy. A strong war movement arose in the United States, although Secretary Bayard wanted a conciliatory policy. But Congress wanted war and appropriated $500,000 to protect American interests in Samoa (some 50 Americans lived there) and $100,000 to build the long delayed naval base at Pago Pago. Three American naval vessels were sent to Samoa and there they stood in the harbor, bristling with guns, facing three German naval vessels. A British cruiser was also in the harbor, sent to protect British interests.

Actually war threatened at any moment, even as the defeated Cleveland administration prepared to relinquish power to the victorious Republicans, and on Inauguration Day one of the questions most vexing to Benjamin Harrison and James G. Blaine, again Secretary of State, was what to do about Samoa.

The problem was resolved, not by diplomats or soldiers, but by nature. A typhoon swept the harbor of Apia on the night of March 15, 1889, and when the weather cleared two days later, not a ship was still afloat. American and German warships were beached or sunk, and only the British man-of-war escaped through the mouth of the harbor.

Undeterred by this affair, which had brought America so near to war over so slight a prospect for imperialist satisfaction, the American *jingoes*, or super-nationalists, continued to grow in strength during the Harrison administration. Francis Ballard Dole led a rebellion in the Hawaiian Islands against the royal government of Queen Liliuokalani, actually assisted by John L. Stevens, the State Department's representative there; and at the end of the Harrison administration preparations were made by the expansionist-minded Republicans to annex Hawaii. As for the rest of American policy under the Harrison administration, it, too, was expansionist and international in outlook. Secretary Blaine succeeded finally in achieving his hemispheric conference in the autumn of 1889, and although the conference was disappointing in its lack of concrete results, from it came the establishment of the Pan-American Union, which for the first time put the 21 American republics in direct communication with one another as a special group. Recognition of this special hemispheric relationship was an important basis for future American foreign policy.

Yet, almost as soon as this basis for friendship was laid, an event occurred which set in motion events that destroyed everything Blaine wished to accomplish in Latin America. During a revolution in Chile in 1891, Minister Patrick Egan gave asylum to some government leaders whose heads were sought by the revolutionaries. When the revolution succeeded, the new government took an unfriendly view of Americans, and when sailors were given shore leave from the *USS Baltimore* in Valparaiso one night, rioting broke out and two Americans were killed and a number were wounded, and 30 were badly beaten by the police and rioters.

At this time, Secretary Blaine was ill, and the matter was handled by Acting Secretary of State William F. Wharton in direct consultation with President Harrison. Wharton's sole qualification for his office of Assistant Secretary of State was a close friendship with Senator Henry Cabot Lodge. One of the problems Blaine faced all through his second period as Secretary was the refusal of President Harrison to allow Blaine to employ men of his own choosing in the State Department, or even to participate in appointments. The policy now followed by the administration was quite contrary to the beliefs of Blaine, but the President was quite obviously being his own Secretary of State. The result was a vinegary correspondence between the State Department and the Chilean foreign ministry, resulting in mutual denunciations before the legislative bodies of the two nations, and a final ultimatum sent to Chile threatening to end diplomatic relations. Worse, before the Chileans had a chance to reply, this was followed by a war message sent by Harrison to Congress. Here was a case of saber rattling and gunboat diplomacy, and the Chileans would not ever forget it. They backed down, but they remembered.

John W. Foster

A few months after this unfortunate occurrence which had destroyed all Blaine set out to accomplish in hemispheric relations, he resigned as Secretary of State, giving no specific reason. He was replaced by John W. Foster, who might almost be called a career diplomat, since he had served as minister to Mexico under President Grant, minister to Russia under President Hayes, minister to Spain under President Arthur, special envoy under President Cleveland, and special envoy handling a seal-fisheries dispute under President Harrison. Foster was not responsible for any innovations of policy, but he managed to clear up all the details of the office. In this last year of the Harrison administration, the President was willing to go slow and so there were no further hurtful outbreaks of jingoism, although the national fever for foreign conquest was rising, prompted by such newspapers as the Pulitzer-owned *New York World* and the Hearst-owned *New York American.*

When the second Cleveland administration took office in the spring of 1893, the Republicans in Congress assumed that the annexation of Hawaii was almost a certain development. Minister Stevens had instituted a virtual American protectorate over Hawaii, and the other nations which had once shown interest in the Sandwich Islands, as they were first called, had backed away, not willing to risk unpleasantness with the saber-rattling Americans over so minor a matter. Cleveland's new Secretary of State, however, happened to be a moralist named Walter Q. Gresham, and Cleveland happened to be anti-imperialist by nature. Gresham and Cleveland received complaints from Queen Liliuokalani that she had been mistreated by the Americans, and they insisted that a special commissioner be sent to Hawaii to ascertain the facts.

When Gresham and Cleveland learned that the queen's rule had been subverted by Americans and that the American

Walter Quintin Gresham

government was deeply involved in the revolution, they refused to continue with moves for annexation. Sentiment in Congress was too strong to be overcome, at this time, and it was apparent that the Hawaiian revolutionaries would not submit to the return of the queen's rule. So the President and Secretary of State did what they could—they stalled and put the matter into the hands of Congress, thus placing responsibility directly on men who did not wish to assume it. There, exactly, is where the Hawaiian question stood at the end of the second Cleveland administration.

Gresham died after little more than two years in office, and was replaced by Richard Olney, who had been Attorney General in the cabinet. Cleveland was much impressed with Olney's handling of the legal aspects of the Hawaiian problem, and the matter that claimed Cleveland's most serious attention, as far as foreign affairs was concerned, was another legal affair involving a disputed boundary in Venezuela. Olney, in Cleveland's opinion, was just the man to handle that problem, and so he was shifted from the Justice Department to the State Department.

The Venezuelan dispute had been going on for 50 years. It involved British and Venezuelan claims concerning the location of the boundary between the South American republic and the colony of British Guiana. Because the United States had enunciated the Monroe Doctrine, a succession of Secretaries of State had been interested in this problem, but by the autumn of 1894 it had become so serious that Britain threatened violence. In his annual message to Congress on December 3 of that year, President Cleveland announced his intention of trying to settle the matter.

The basic problem was the intransigeance of Great Britain. This period marked the height of British colonial power, and the British government did not feel like being told what to do

Richard Olney

by anyone. Cleveland and his Secretaries of State (Gresham and then Olney) suggested arbitration. The British refused arbitration. Spurred by Secretary Olney, Cleveland then joined the saber rattlers, believing that this was the only method of dealing with a bellicose Great Britain. He proposed that the United States provide expenses for a boundary commission to examine the facts of the case. After the report was made and accepted by the American government, the United States would stick to the report, and if Britain tried to appropriate territory that the report gave to Venezuela, then there would be war. Cleveland and Olney prepared this message and gave it to Congress on December 17, 1895, just a little more than a year after the President had vowed to use his best efforts to settle this matter under the aegis of the Monroe Doctrine.

Congress applauded; it was in a fighting mood.

The British had gone a long way on the road to war, but at that point they faced problems in South Africa, where the Boers were taking matters into their own hands, with moral support by German Kaiser Wilheim II, who had his own reasons for wanting Britain's wings clipped. So Britain decided it was more important to fight in South Africa than in Venezuela; the boundary dispute was settled, and the Monroe Doctrine survived a major test. The dignity of the declaration had been in question; after the Venezuelan boundary dispute its status was no longer doubtful, for the United States had stepped in to help a native American republic without serving any selfish North American interest. So the second Cleveland administration ended in a burst of foreign-policy glory.

Foreign affairs seemed to be a matter of little importance to William McKinley, who became President in the spring of 1897, otherwise, he would not have chosen poor old Senator

John Sherman as Secretary of State. Sherman was long past his prime. He was 74 years old, and even older than his years. The reason for his selection was plain to all the world: McKinley's president maker, Mark Hanna, wanted Sherman's Ohio Senate seat. He got it, and the United States got an incompetent Secretary of State.

It made little difference, however. McKinley had his own ideas, and he proposed to exercise the office through William R. Day, the Assistant Secretary, who was his crony from Ohio. Matters were to be cut and dried between them, and Secretary Sherman was simply to lend his great national prestige to the transactions. Hawaii was to be annexed; indeed, a representative of the Hawaiian Republic had come to Washington before the McKinley inauguration to settle the details. (Hawaii was annexed by a treaty which was signed on June 16, 1897.)

That fall and in the winter of 1898, Secretary Sherman began dragging his heels, especially in regard to the longing eyes American newspapers and the administration were casting on Cuba. He was forgetful (he once told the Japanese that the United States was not even *contemplating* the annexation of Hawaii). He was very much opposed to the imperialism he saw around him in the cabinet and in high office, especially to the spur-jangling of Assistant Secretary of the Navy, Theodore Roosevelt, who wanted to send the American navy everywhere at once. Roosevelt hoped to infuriate Spain and get into war with her, and Sherman knew it and disapproved.

In January, 1898, when the American consul in Havana reported to Washington on unrest in Cuba and asked for warships to come and calm matters down by their presence, American policy was discussed and, in spite of Sherman's opposition, McKinley decided to send naval vessels into Cuban waters. The battleship *Maine* was sent to Havana. On the

John Sherman

night of February 15, she exploded in Havana harbor and 250 sailors died.

Out of this all came an investigation, a rush to send the battleship *Oregon* around Cape Horn to Atlantic waters, and a realization that American policies, naval, military and foreign, must be drastically changed if sabers were to be rattled any more. The problems were that the American navy was small and its ships were old and outmoded. The army was also small and its weapons were obsolete. The foreign policy, geared to the Monroe Doctrine and vestiges of Washingtonian isolationism, was outmoded for a nation that wanted foreign territory, lots of it, to match the acquisitions of the other powers of the world.

In the cabinet dispute over Cuba and war, Secretary Sherman showed his strong character; he resigned, and Secretary Day continued the work he had begun.

At the end of the Spanish-American War the United States acquired all the territories, and woes, that it wanted, if not more. Cuba was rejected as an American possession in a moment of revulsion against colonialism in the Western Hemisphere, but, on the other hand, America acquired Puerto Rico and Guam and bought the Philippines.

McKinley then had second thoughts about imperialism. He appointed William Howard Taft to head the commission that was to bring peace and security to the Philippines, largely because Taft was opposed to the idea of having the Philippines in the first place. He appointed John Hay as Secretary of State, and Hay was notable as the man who carried out the Open Door policy toward China.

In the 1890's, the European powers and Japan were busily carving up China into spheres of influence and even colonies. The Germans took Kiaochow as a colony, the Russians held much of Manchuria, the British had Hong Kong, the Portuguese held Macao, and the French were moving toward

William R. Day

colonization of several southern provinces. In the Boxer Rebellion of 1900 and afterwards, the United States took the position that China must not be cut up, that her territory should be preserved and her power to govern it, too, and that all the world should have equal trade rights with the Chinese empire.

Secretary Hay served under McKinley, and then under Theodore Roosevelt after McKinley's assassination in 1901. Hay was responsible for the Hay-Pauncefote Treaty, which did away with the Clayton-Bulwer Treaty and allowed the United States to build the Panama Canal. Hay then supervised the delicate negotiations—carried on with Panama and Nicaragua separately—until they became most indelicate. Theodore Roosevelt was not a sensitive fellow, and he usually followed a direct line between two points. Consequently, after Panama refused to accept the treaty with the United States calling for the building of a canal in Panama, a revolution occurred in Panama and the United States troops, in "protecting" the canal lines of communication, kept a body of soldiers from nearby Colombia from putting down the revolution. When the revolutionary government came to power, presto, a very favorable treaty for America was produced. In Latin America, they called it the "rape of Panama" and Secretary Hay was held as much responsible for it as President Theodore Roosevelt. It was unfair to blame Hay— he was the servant of his President, and Roosevelt had his own way all through the affair. Hay had not even wanted to deal with Panama, but preferred to put the canal through Nicaragua.

It really would not have made much difference who succeeded Hay as Secretary of State in the Roosevelt cabinet, except from the standpoint of administrative competence. In this regard, Roosevelt was fortunate, after Hay died, in having Elihu Root to call upon. Root was a lawyer and a states-

John Hay

man. He brought in the foreign-service examinations and the process of merit promotion within the department. He advocated sizable allowances for rent and other expenses for foreign service officers, trying to make the diplomatic corps as attractive as possible to bright people. He also tried to mend relations with Latin America, which were in a sad state of disrepair, made the first Good Will trip South, and persuaded Andrew Carnegie to finance the building of the Pan American Union building in Washington, which was donated to all the 21 American republics.

Having risen to heights of imperialism, the United States was taken very seriously by the nations of Europe during the last days of the Roosevelt administration, far more seriously as a power than ever before.

In two conferences at The Hague, Secretary Root proposed the establishment of an international court of justice. He succeeded, before he was through, in mending some of the tears in the inter-American fabric caused by gunboat diplomacy, but his most salient achievements were in securing respect for American policies in Europe and Asia. He stood strongly for arbitration of international disputes and concluded some 25 treaties with various nations calling for arbitration, leading among other things to settlement of the longstanding northeastern fisheries dispute with Great Britain.

Except for an interim appointment of an assistant, for a few weeks in 1909, Root was succeeded in the Secretariat by Philander C. Knox, who was President Taft's chief foreign officer. The foreign policy of the Taft administration was notable for reorganization of the State Department, which had grown large and unwieldy, and for "dollar diplomacy," which was little other than use of the growing supply of American capital to consolidate the position of world power

Elihu Root

Philander C. Knox

developed by the McKinley and Roosevelt administrations.

In the reorganization, the department came out with 35 officers, 135 clerks, and a dozen service employees, such as telephone operators and porters. There were many innovations to be faced, including a growing volume of American tourists abroad. In 1910, some 25,000 Americans traveled abroad, requiring passports, while ten years earlier only 14,-000 had traveled abroad, and in the middle of the nineteenth century just a handful had gone abroad for their own purposes.

The matter of dollar diplomacy was an indication of the growth of American economic power, for Secretary Knox and President Taft set out openly to use United States dollars to strengthen American positions. An American representative was sent to China as a member of an international banking group, and he tried to secure neutralization of the Manchurian railways. Russia and Japan, which ran them, stopped that *détente,* but it was a good try. Much of the good done by Elihu Root was wiped out in the open use of American money to expand American interests in the Latin American countries, not always in the long-range interests of the countries involved.

And so the American policy of imperialism was born, burgeoned and was brought under control in the years between 1884 and 1912, leaving behind it some flickering remnants such as the use of economic power to achieve foreign policy ends. This use of capital was to continue on a private basis for a long time, and was to cause the United States, years later, alone among world powers to be accused of perpetrating and perpetuating economic imperialism. The idea, talked about so loudly in the 1950's and 1960's, was a true representation of an American policy, but of the policy of a half century earlier; and in those days dollar diplomacy was regarded as a virtue, not a vice.

The New Isolationism

When Woodrow Wilson was elected President of the United States in 1912, the matter of foreign policy seemed to be of little significance. The world was as peaceful as it had ever been, and American eyes were turned very much inward. The state of affairs that existed is perhaps best illustrated by Wilson's appointment of his first Secretary of State. He chose William Jennings Bryan, the man who had been Democratic candidate for President three times in the past, and the man who still commanded the loyalty of almost half the Democratic party. Bryan had many different qualifications, but he did not have either an interest in or an aptitude for conducting foreign relations.

Wilson intended to assume responsibility for the conduct of foreign relations himself. As we have seen, all strong Presidents did likewise, but the other strong Presidents chose men of clerical or administrative bend to carry out their policies. Wilson chose a character as strong as himself, and a man of entirely different background and belief. Take one very small point: Secretary Bryan was a teetotaller, one of such conviction about the evils of alcohol that he served grape juice instead of wine at state dinners. European diplomats, who had grown up on wines, could not understand this prejudice, and the French Ambassador was openly contemptuous of the Secretary of State.

Bryan considered his most important contribution would be to work out a plan for promotion of peace through treaty. He tried to secure the adherence of all countries to a Treaty for the Advancement of Peace, under which all nations would agree to submit unsettled disputes to investigation by impartial commissions.

President Wilson, for his part, quickly assumed the mantle of director of foreign relations. One of his earliest statements, made in the cabinet meeting of March 11, 1913, declared flatly that the United States had nothing to gain in Central or South America and that dollar diplomacy must be eliminated. Yet he did not eliminate the dollar diplomacy at all, but he carried it farther than his Republican predecessors. The record shows that the United States used troops and invaded Latin American countries with greater frequency in the Wilson administration than in any other.

The Wilson administration was peculiar in one sense: the State Department ceased for the time being to be the basic instrument of foreign-policy control. Odd as that sounds, it was true. The President simply did not trust the conservative career foreign service officers and preferred not to use them to carry out his policies. An example of the strange situation and the convoluted diplomacy that resulted from it was the case of Mexico. In 1911, the government of President Porfirio Díaz had finally fallen, as a result of a coup in which American ambassador Henry Lane Wilson was involved. Victoriano de la Huerta was installed as President of Mexico.

William Jennings Bryan

Britain recognized the government. Germany recognized it. So did nearly all other countries. But the United States refused to recognize the government because President Wilson and Secretary Bryan disapproved of a government that was founded by force. They also knew that Huerta was detested by the liberals and the leftists of the Americas. The Mexican government of President Huerta did not represent the people, they said, and they refused to deal with it. Instead of working through normal diplomatic channels, President Wilson sent his friend William Bayard Hale to Mexico, and Bryan sent his friend John Lind. The American attitude brought about the alienation of this Huerta Mexican government and the alienation of a large part of Latin America because of what the other peoples in the Americas regarded as a high-handed *norteamericano* policy. This unique attitude toward *recognition* of governments was to become an integral part of American foreign policy and would hamper United States dealings with the rest of the world for the next half century. As of this writing, the policy persists, notably in relation to Communist China, whose government rules the most populous nation in the world yet is not recognized as a government at all by the United States.

Disapproval of Mexico became so severe that in 1914 American troops went ashore at Vera Cruz and occupied the customs house there. Eventually, the Huerta regime fell, and Huerta and his family fled to the Caribbean aboard a German warship, but the American interference in Mexican affairs was not forgotten.

Nor was Mexico the sole example of American interference and use of force. Haiti was occupied by the United States marines in 1915, who remained there for 19 years. The Dominican Republic, on the other half of the same island, was occupied by marines until 1924.

In the beginning, President Wilson made appointments to the Department of State. Bryan wanted to "give the faithful a chance"—to use State Department posts to pay political debts, but Wilson countermanded that decision, and made some effort to find suitable men. It was a difficult task, because Bryan was not well-regarded in the community of well-to-do intellectuals, and several men that Wilson wanted, such as former Secretary of State Richard Olney, found that it was inconvenient for them to join the administration. Most career diplomats in high places were removed: of the 40 major missions, 29 were changed in the first six months of the new administration. The Wilson-Bryan policy was not new; political changes would always follow change of party administration in the United States. But such a policy would always deny any credence to talk about bipartisanship in foreign policy.

There were outright cases of dishonesty and fraud in the foreign service at this time. The most notorious of these concerned a Democratic politician named James M. Sullivan. He was appointed minister to the Dominican Republic after the American marines moved in. It was soon discovered that Minister Sullivan represented gambling interests in New York. Bryan called Sullivan a "strong, courageous, reliable fellow," but a subsequent investigation revealed that Sullivan had exceeded his instructions while minister, involved himself in Dominican politics, obtained concessions for his friends, and had gone heavily into debt in the Dominican Republic.

Secretary Bryan had some peculiar ideas about the position of a cabinet officer, too. For many years he had earned money as a Chautauqua speaker, making regular speeches for pay on the circuit conducted by the Chautauqua organization. After Bryan joined the cabinet, he still spoke for pay, and thus offended both professional diplomats and public organizations. It was charged that he spent so much time away from Washington on personal business that he could not possibly know what was happening in the Department of State.

Almost immediately after the new administration came to office, the professionals began to resign from the State Department. In furtherance of the Open Door policy in China, an international consortium of bankers had banded together to finance Chinese government activities. This consortium was vital to the independence of the Chinese government. Wilson and Bryan did not see the need for American support of China, however, and withdrew the government's backing of the banking arrangement. Two weeks after taking office, without consulting the professionals of the State Department, Wilson and Bryan announced the end of the arrangement. The experienced Assistant Secretary of State, Huntington Wilson, resigned as a result of this move, not so much because the policy was changed, but because it was changed without serious considerations being given to the policy and without seeking the advice of experts.

Soon the State Department's experts were leaving, resigning, or being pushed out to make way for political appointees. Assistant Secretary Huntington Wilson was replaced by a man whose claim to competence in the field of foreign affairs was based on his membership in the Democratic National Committee. The Third Assistant Secretary of State was Dudley Field Malone, a New York lawyer who knew nothing about diplomacy. A businessman took over direction of the division of Latin American affairs. A law professor took over the Division of Near Eastern Affairs. Two new foreign trade advisors were appointed: a former private secretary of Bryan's and a presidential elector from Kentucky.

In the spring and summer of 1914, Secretary Bryan con-

Robert Lansing

cerned himself with his treaties of peace, which were, he said, bound to assure international amity for generations to come. Some 20 of these treaties were drawn up and sent to the United States Senate for approval by July. The next month, war threatened in Europe.

With the threat of a general war, President Wilson began to understand that his foreign policies were deficient and that the State Department had become so weakened that it was a target for abuse of the opposition press. The department was so badly undermined and demoralized that the diplomats abroad had not even warned the government at home of the danger of war, although all during July little else had been discussed in the chanceries of Europe. The European crisis came as very much a surprise to the Americans in Washington; only Ambassador Myron T. Herrick seemed to realize the seriousness of the situation; and when he asked Secretary Bryan to try to mediate the difference between Austria and Serbia, it was July 28, far too late for any effective action to be taken in behalf of peace.

When war broke out three days later, Secretary Bryan seemed to lose interest in the Department of State altogether. He spent more and more of his time on speaking tours, and the operation of the department was left largely to Robert Lansing, counselor of the State Department, who served as Acting Secretary.

At this time a strange situation developed: with Bryan's long absences, President Wilson and his aide, Colonel House, began to exercise a foreign policy that was quite different from the State Department policy, and various ambassadors followed policies of their own choosing. Thus, Lansing's concern was with the announced neutrality of the United States. Great Britain violated that neutrality in a number of ways, and Lansing was inclined to protest these violations in harsh language. But Colonel House met independently with Sir Cecil Spring-Rice and toned down the protests. Businessmen also pursued the most un-neutral of policies, and in 1915 the J. P. Morgan bank began financing the British and some of the French war effort.

By the spring of 1915, President Wilson and Secretary Bryan were poles apart in their attitude toward the war. Wilson had sent Colonel House to Europe as his special emissary to try to bring an end to the war. Bryan had objected to House's going instead of himself, whereupon Wilson had told Bryan that the mission was "unofficial." At the same time, the President told Colonel House that he was to report directly to the President, and that the President would act through him to "avoid all intermediaries." Secretary Bryan, in other words, was being circumvented.

One reason for this circumvention was the difference in attitude toward the belligerent powers. President Wilson was horrified by the German development of submarine warfare. Secretary Bryan felt the British were carrying on equally improper actions, particularly in seizure of American ships, and he disapproved of the financing of the British war effort in America and the American sale of munitions to Britain.

On February 15, the Germans had warned Americans against traveling on British ships in the war zone. Secretary Bryan had wanted to prohibit Americans from traveling on belligerent ships of any nation, but the President would not agree. Then, on May 7, the British liner *Lusitania* was sunk by a German submarine, and 124 Americans were drowned. Colonel House was in London, and he urged that President Wilson join the war on the side of the Allies. Ambassador Walter Hines Page joined him. President Wilson drew a strong note of protest to Germany without consulting Bryan or anyone else in the State Department, and read it to a meeting of his cabinet. Bryan alone objected to the harshness of the protest. The President promised that he would make a supplementary statement warning Americans against traveling on belligerent ships, and Bryan agreed to sign the protest note as Secretary of State.

But then President Wilson reneged on his agreement to send a secondary statement. In conversation with the Austrian ambassador, Bryan was so unfortunate as to indicate that the *Lusitania* note was for home consumption and need not be taken too seriously by Germany, and the Austrian ambassador told the Germans, who told the world. Bryan was misquoted, but his discomfiture at the whole proceeding was known, and his relations with President Wilson suffered greatly because of the incident.

The Germans replied offensively to the protest on the *Lusitania*, and President Wilson was furious. In cabinet meetings, he and Bryan clashed because Bryan insisted that the British be assigned some blame for the incident. The President used harsh words to squelch his Secretary of State.

Relations then were nearly at an end. Bryan returned to the State Department and wrote several letters to the President asking him to change his position regarding neutrality, but the President was moving swiftly to the side of the Allies and would not be swayed. Bryan resigned as Secretary of State on June 9, 1915, citing the differences between himself and the President over war policy. He resigned, knowing that he was bringing his long political career to an end, for in quitting the cabinet under such conditions he was, for all practical purposes, reading himself out of the Democratic party and national politics. Bryan resigned none the less, largely as a matter of principle, but also partly because of Wilson's insistence on making major decisions of foreign policy without consulting with his Secretary of State.

From the beginning it was almost inevitable that the resignation would come with any important developments in American foreign policy, because it was quite impossible for two such strong-minded men to work together for any period of time under stress. The Bryan case was simply proof again that ultimately foreign policy is the responsibility of the President as Chief Executive of the United States, and that his Secretary of State and all other officers of the department can be no more than advisers and servants if the President is doing his job.

The New Internationalism

On Secretary Bryan's resignation, President Wilson moved to correct error by appointing Robert Lansing as Secretary. Lansing's position and turn of mind are well indicated in random comments that accompanied the presidential request. "He is only a clerk," said Mrs. Bolling, the lady the President intended to marry. Lansing himself said he had too little political influence to warrant the appointment.

Lansing was exactly the kind of man that could best serve President Wilson in the post of Secretary of State since the President wished to make foreign policy all by himself. But Lansing was more than a clerk; he had been a counselor of the department, he was a lawyer, and he was the son-in-law of John W. Foster, who had been Secretary of State himself.

As to his political influence, or lack of it, the President indicated that what he wanted was a trained technician— and that was what he was getting. Count von Bernstorff, the German Ambassador to Washington, summed up the situation in the State Department when he said that an interview with

173

Secretary Lansing was simply a matter of form because the President decided everything himself. But that remark does not tell the whole story of what happened in the department. With the departure of Secretary Bryan, the department began to settle down to become more useful in reporting and negotiating than it had been in the first days of the administration.

Aside from the European war into which the United States was most certainly drifting, the most important aspect of American policy in the years after 1915 was in regard to Latin America. So much work was occasioned by the Mexican revolution that a special division of Mexican affairs was established. Yet the President continued to handle policy himself, and did not do a very good job of it. General Venustiano Carranza gained control of southern Mexico and northern Mexico was held by Emiliano Zapata and Pancho Villa, a pair of guerrilla leaders who were often called bandits. Wilson thought all the various revolutionary leaders could be brought together (which showed his basic misunderstanding of the processes of revolution). Carranza refused flatly, saying that he represented the legal government and would not compromise with bandits. Finally, in October, 1915, President Wilson decided to recognize the Carranza regime, but by this time, the others had gained enough power so that it took two years for the revolution to settle down. In that period, all three revolutionary leaders were assassinated, but before he died Pancho Villa managed to bring the United States army marching again into Mexico by murdering a number of American citizens. Once again, the Americans gained a bad reputation with Latin Americans because of physical intervention in Mexican affairs, although the outcome was actually salutary. Carranza had brought a new constitution for Mexico into being, and his successor, Alvaro Obregón, would rule a legal state. The revolution was ended, and historians gave Wilson a good deal of credit for helping end it satisfactorily. Thus Wilson's policies, like much of American policy toward Latin America, were ambiguous in the extreme.

During the heat of the Mexican troubles came the presidential election of 1916, and one might say that the second Wilson term, which began on March 4, 1917, was an entirely different administration than that of 1912 as far as American foreign policy was concerned. Wilson tried, within four short years, to change the United States, and himself, from an isolationist view of world affairs to an almost visionary internationalist view. The nation would follow him most of the way, and some of the nation would follow him all the way, but in the end the change would be too drastic, coming too fast, and the President would suffer a great defeat.

In the summer of 1916, after the *Lusitania* sinking and other incidents, the feeling in America toward the war began to change. Theodore Roosevelt led the pro-war party, which transcended normal political party lines in its demands for intervention. Former Secretary Bryan spoke out against preparedness, but Wilson took up the case for war preparations, and the nation generally agreed with him, although the people were not yet ready for war. At the Democratic National Convention of 1916, Wilson was praised because he had kept America out of war. But sentiment changed rapidly, and during the last stages of the election campaign against Republican Charles Evans Hughes it became apparent that sentiment was moving toward the Roosevelt interventionist position.

Wilson made one heroic attempt to mediate the war, and the Germans simultaneously indicated a willingness to negotiate peace; but the Germans insisted on retaining some of the territory they had captured, and the attempt came to nothing.

Secretary Lansing had some influence on the Wilson change in position. As early as the summer of 1915, he had begun writing memos to the President declaring that the Germans must not be allowed to impose a *Pax Germanica* on the world, even though to prevent German victory the United States might have to enter the war. Lansing was most effective in his arguments because he never allowed his own disagreements with the President's neutrality policy to show in cabinet meetings or anywhere else, except in private. He gained a reputation in the cabinet of simply parroting the President, when in fact he was doing his utmost, with some success, to bring Wilson around to an interventionist position. There was a lesson in Lansing's way of doing things for future Secretaries of State who might serve strong Presidents.

As far as American war policy was concerned, the most important factor was the German submarine warfare. In this war, the Germans inaugurated an entirely new concept. Until World War I and even in the beginning of the war, warships capturing civilian vessels always warned the captains and the crews, and always either gave them opportunity to escape by small boat or delivered them eventually to neutral ports. But with the development of the submarine and the high-speed torpedo, surprise became an important factor in naval warfare, and the niceties of war rules passed into history. The United States was very much concerned about the continued German sinking of passenger vessels and the loss of civilian lives. Early in 1916, when a German submarine sank a French channel steamer, Secretary Lansing wrote a note to Wilson, urging the severance of diplomatic relations with Germany. The President was not ready. He toned down the protest. But there were signs that he was listening to his Secretary.

The Germans brought about the American entrance into

the war, taking a calculated risk, and knowing what they were doing. After the long struggle at the Marne, as early as 1915, some German leaders realized that they would never win the victory they had expected. By the end of 1916, it became apparent that the war was stalemated, and that if the United States brought its power to bear on the side of the Allies, Germany was lost. But there was, said the admirals and the generals, one chance: It was to make submarine warfare even more frightful, and starve England into submission before the United States could act. So Count von Bernstorff, on the last day of January, 1917, informed Secretary Lansing that beginning the next day all ships entering a war zone marked out around Britain, France and Italy would be sunk without notice.

Lansing decided that the only course he could recommend was to break off relations with Germany immediately. He went to the White House and advised the President accordingly. So careful had Lansing been in the past to accommodate President Wilson's language and manners while pressing his own ideas, that his plea was very effective. Wilson was convinced. For two more months, the United States hesitated to declare war, so ingrained was the distaste for involvement. But on April 6, war was declared, the Senate voting for it 82 to 6 and the House of Representatives 375 to 50, clearly reflecting the great change in the climate of the nation.

In spite of President Wilson's trust and use of Secretary Lansing as an effective instrument of foreign policy, the President still did not use the State Department as his major tool. A special organization was established in New York, under Colonel House, to consider the coming peace treaty. When President Wilson decided on a plan for a League of Nations, the State Department was not even consulted. The armistice ending the war was signed on November 11, 1918, and in less than a month the American commission left for Paris. As of that moment, the President had not consulted with his Secretary of State on the subject, had not shown him the plan, or even told him that a plan had been prepared. The entire plan, and Wilson's famous Fourteen Points for peace were prepared by Colonel House and the special commission.

As the Peace Conference time came near, President Wilson announced that he intended to go to Paris to act as his own foreign minister in working out the peace. Secretary Lansing objected, but he quickly realized that his objections were not welcome. Wilson was determined to do the job himself, although he would take Lansing along as a member of the delegation. And even at Paris, the State Department group of experts and delegates was overshadowed by Colonel House's special commission.

Obviously, this ignoring of the department caused resentments, and it is here that the breakdown of relations between Wilson and his very useful and intelligent Secretary of State began. In the earliest days of the Paris meeting, Secretary Lansing instructed his department officials that they ought to prepare a draft treaty which could be used as a basis for discussion among the American representatives at least. President Wilson took exception to Lansing's action, and told him to desist; he did not propose to have lawyers drafting the treaty, he said. Lansing was the only lawyer involved, and the remark was obviously aimed at him alone.

The State Department and the Secretary were virtually ignored in all the work done at Paris by the Americans, a fact which could not be prevented from becoming known to the rest of the world and unavoidably lessened the State Department's position in international affairs. One reason that the State Department was overlooked was that Lansing and his President were of different minds about the details of the peace treaty; consequently, the President paid no attention to his Secretary of State. Lansing addressed a number of letters and memoranda to the President, and almost uniformly they went unanswered. Lansing had lost the confidence of his chief.

When the Treaty of Versailles was signed, Secretary Lansing came back to the United States and spoke in favor of it, and worked in favor of it; but relations between the Secretary and the President grew steadily worse. Lansing was accused by William C. Bullitt, one of the men on House's commission, of saying that the treaty was a bad one, the League of Nations was a bad idea, and that the Senate ought to vote down the treaty. Lansing denied making this statement, but Wilson believed he had made it.

Lansing's final downfall was brought about by an issue of a kind that would confront the nation again less than half a century later. In the autumn of 1920, President Wilson became totally incapacitated by illness, but the extent of his illness was concealed from the American people. Secretary Lansing made an attempt to have the President's illness noted publicly, so that Vice-President Thomas R. Marshall might take over direction of the government and carry on the orderly processes. The decision that this was *not* to be done was made by two relatively unimportant figures, Joseph Tumulty, secretary to the President, and the White House physician, Grayson. The government of the United States, on a policy level, came to a standstill and threatened to remain that way.

But even though the President of the United States was incapacitated, life and the world went on, and Secretary Lansing, a man of considerable courage, took matters into his own hands. He consulted privately with Secretary of War Newton D. Baker and Secretary of the Interior Franklin K.

Lane, and called meetings of the cabinet to discuss important official business. During a period of about four months, America was governed by committee.

In February, a recuperating President Wilson took violent objection to the meetings, and called on Lansing to explain. Lansing said he had called the cabinet to discuss matters that could not be delayed, but that if the President thought he had acted unconstitutionally he would resign. Wilson accused Lansing of assuming presidential authority and accepted his resignation immediately, but Wilson was not entirely open with his explanations. He charged Lansing, and Lansing only, with disloyalty, although other members of the cabinet had participated in the action. Navy Secretary Josephus Daniels suggested that the real reason for the accusation was that Lansing had issued an ultimatum to Mexico, because an American consular agent had been captured and held there by bandits. The Secretary of State had not consulted the President or the cabinet in issuing the ultimatum, and Wilson was angry, said Daniels.

Perhaps that is part of the reason for Lansing's departure, but at best it could be considered to be *only* part of it. The handwriting was on the wall at Paris when the President ignored his chief foreign policy officer. Part of the explanation must be that as Lansing gained experience and knowledge he felt that he had a right to utilize these, and President Wilson wanted a State Department clerk for Secretary, not a strong figure in his own right.

President Wilson's insistence on having his own way entirely caused the Versailles Treaty and the League of Nations to fail passage in the United States Senate. Lansing would have made the concessions necessary for passage, and so would have Vice-President Marshall. But Wilson was a proud and self-destructive man in 1919 and 1920, and his use of

Bainbridge Colby

power shaped the future of America and of the world in a warped pattern.

Lansing was replaced as Secretary of State by Bainbridge Colby, a lawyer who was selected for his administrative abilities and his willingness to take orders rather than his experience in diplomatic affairs, for he had none. It was apparent that President Wilson intended to continue his personal management of American foreign relations.

In the spring of 1920, President Wilson had recovered from his illness—later revealed as arteriosclerosis and a stroke that paralyzed his left arm and leg—at least enough to carry on his office and make decisions about foreign affairs.

Colby was to enunciate one more important policy for President Wilson, a repetition of his policy toward the Huerta regime of Mexico. When the occasion arose to discuss American policy toward the new Soviet revolutionary government of Russia, Colby announced that the United States would not recognize the Soviet Union because the United States disapproved of the international revolutionary nature of the regime. That policy was to be followed by the United States for the next 13 years and to retain a definite influence on American attitudes toward Russia and other Communist lands for a half century.

In the administrative or routine matters of foreign affairs, Bainbridge Colby made an excellent record during his single year in office. He repaired some of the damage done to American-Mexican relations in the few years before his term, and he gave a new interpretation of the Monroe Doctrine, reaffirming the American belief in the right to self-government of all the American peoples and the determination of the United States to protect the Western Hemisphere from outsiders.

The election campaign of 1920 was waged largely on the

issue of foreign policy, with President Wilson insisting that the issues be the League of Nations and the Versailles Treaty. The Democrats lost the election, the Republicans won it, and an entirely new direction in foreign policy was in the offing, as anyone could see in the autumn of 1920. The spring of 1921 would bring the change.

In Splendid Isolation

The election of 1920 brought into office an administration that had no interest at all in foreign affairs. President Warren G. Harding could consider his isolationist position to be justified by the huge plurality of the vote that he obtained, since the League of Nations was the basic issue of the election.

So the United States went into a period of isolation from the affairs of the world, having spent the last half dozen years thoroughly immersed in world problems. Some Republican leaders had supported a plan for a modified League of Nations, but their idea was discarded in the post-election planning, and their internationalist candidate for Secretary of State, Elihu Root, was ignored by President Harding in favor of Charles Evans Hughes, a man of great presence and tremendous dignity, although not a man normally associated with foreign affairs.

Many factors interplayed to create this appointment, and not the least of them was the belief of a small group of senators led by Henry Cabot Lodge that they could exert more influence on the conduct of foreign relations under this administration than had been normal for legislators in the past. President Harding and Secretary Hughes quickly established the proper relationship, however. The President told newspaper reporters that in the future they would get their information about foreign affairs from the State Department. The Secretary quickly let the senators know that he intended to be Secretary of State and that he would brook little congressional interference in appointments.

The situation of the State Department, beginning in 1921, was quite the reverse of what it had been since 1913. Instead of being responsible almost directly to a strong and vigorous President who insisted on being his own Secretary of State, the department was responsible to the Secretary. Instead of being kept out in the cold and ignored in connection with vital matters of foreign policy, the State Department was the hub of American foreign policy, and it was to be administered largely by career diplomats. The most remarkable change inaugurated by Secretary Hughes was to bring into Washington a large number of these experts. He chose an Undersecretary of State, who would serve as chief administrative officer of the department under his orders. He was Henry P. Fletcher, a long-time diplomat. There were three assistant Secretaries of State, two of them diplomats and the third a long-time adviser to Secretaries of State. Career officers were brought in as chiefs of the various geographical divisions into which the ever-growing State Department was divided: Far Eastern Affairs; Latin American Affairs, etc.

In essence, the department was thoroughly reorganized. This change came about partly because a Republican administration replaced a Democratic regime, but there was a more basic reason. Under President Wilson's policy of using

Charles Evans Hughes

outside advisers, the strength of the State Department had diminished, and it needed rebuilding.

When the department was rebuilt, it became a smoothly functioning machine that set the pattern of relations with the press for the modern State Department in the beginning of the second half of the twentieth century. Because of the peculiar nature of his position, Secretary Lansing had been elusive in his dealings with the press. Before him, Bryan had been absent a good deal of the time, and after him Bainbridge Colby was simply exercising a caretaker role in behalf of an ailing President who insisted on acting like a Secretary of State. Secretary Hughes began a policy of press conferences, twice every working day, and either he or Undersecretary Fletcher would attend to give information and answer questions.

The diplomatic policies of Secretary Hughes and President Harding, however, were far more conservative and isolationist than the administrative policy of adaptation of modern machinery of government and the use of trained personnel.

Two high points emerged in this administration. They were the serious attempt to limit the war-making potential of the great powers and a revised and almost turn-about policy toward Latin America.

Oddly enough, the impetus for the first came from one of the strongest isolationist senators in Congress, William E. Borah of Idaho. He suggested the policy in a resolution in the Senate because he believed the United States was spending too much money on naval armament. The administration at first looked askance at the proposal, and then began to see merit in it, and the British seemed to be working in the same direction. So Secretary Hughes gave out a press release that the United States had issued invitations for a conference on limitation of armaments and on matters relating to Far Eastern affairs. The conference was held in Washington for three months, beginning in November, 1921.

Secretary Hughes took the initiative in these discussions and achieved an agreement called the 5–5–3 ratio of armament, which meant five capital ships (battleships) for the United States, and five such ships for Great Britain to every three ships for Japan.

Tied to this treaty very closely was the Nine-Power Treaty, which was worked out at about the same time, calling for the respect of the territorial integrity of China. During World War I, Japan had attacked and driven out the German colonists in Kiaochow, but had then decided to keep most of Shantung province for herself. Secretary Hughes secured the return of Shantung to China and the acceptance of America's Open Door policy, which had been languishing in recent years.

Secretary Hughes stopped a war between Costa Rica and Panama over boundary problems by asking for arbitration, and when the Panamanians refused arbitration, he brought forth his big stick and said the United States would use force, if necessary, to settle the boundary dispute. He repaired relations with Mexico to some extent by recognizing President Obregón's government after the Mexicans had promised not to confiscate the property of American citizens. He caused the overdue withdrawal of the marines from the Dominican Republic, too, and his most important declarations of policy relative to Latin America were those in which he promised protection of peace and non-interference in Latin American affairs.

In certain ways one could not really say that the United States was following a policy of isolation—if isolation means solely to remain apart from the rest of the world. In its own way, America in this period was most seriously concerned with foreign peoples and most generous with them. Massive relief programs were brought to Europe and the Near East by American groups. To be sure, these were groups supported partly, but not altogether, by private charity. Herbert Hoover's American Relief Association was heavily supported by the government, although Near East Relief was totally a private affair.

Again, the strange Puritanical attitude toward governments of which the United States government disapproved was exhibited by the Harding administration, and later, after Harding's death, by the Coolidge administration. Secretary Hughes continued in office, and he saw no reason to change the policy laid down by President Wilson toward the Union of Soviet Socialist Republics. The most cogent reason given was that the USSR was dedicated to the subversion of the United States and its institutions, and few Americans even attempted to argue against that point. But here was a growing Russia on the one hand, and a growing America on the other, and by refusing recognition, the United States lost whatever chance there might have been to influence the development of the younger, weaker nation.

The basic reason that the America of the 1920's and 1930's earned the title of isolationist, however, was in its refusal to deal with the League of Nations, whose membership comprised all the important powers of the world and most of the unimportant ones. For the first six months of the Harding administration, neither State Department nor President even answered letters sent by that body to the United States government. Eventually the letters were acknowledged, but that was about all the attention that was given them. The Europeans were disgusted that the nation whose President had done so much to establish the League would not participate, and, faced with this rudeness, the League members became annoyed, and America's position of aloofness was sometimes overstated.

In this policy, Secretary of State Hughes was not following his own bent, which was international. He had been one of the Republican leaders to back limited support of the League of Nations before 1920. But Secretary Hughes recognized the facts of political life and, in the early 1920's, the facts were that the isolationist cabal of senators was in control of Congress and had a large backing by the American public. Secretary Hughes did what he could to retain contact with the League, sending unofficial observers to various meetings, and advocating American adherence to the Permanent Court of International Justice to be established at The Hague. The Dawes plan for reparations payments by Germany was developed by Hughes and Vice-President Dawes.

When speaking of isolationism, one can scarcely place the blame on either the Harding or Coolidge administration, for the American public was largely responsible for the basic tenor of foreign policy. The public pushed the Washington Naval Conference by its approval during the formative period when the idea was under discussion. The public approved American aid abroad, both private, and, to a less extent, public. The public also wanted to scrimp and save government money, and the result was a series of economy budgets for the Department of State. In 1921, the department had 714 employees, and in 1923 that number had been reduced to 590, while the work load expected of the department had increased by almost 25 percent. But the public, in the 1920's, was greatly concerned with the development of the private segment of the American economy, and little concerned with the public segment. All government suffered in this regard.

After the election of Calvin Coolidge as President in his

own right, Secretary Hughes decided to resign. And when he made his decision, for once the public and press were quick to realize that in the person of Secretary Hughes they had enjoyed the services of perhaps the strongest Secretary of State in the history of the nation. He had presided over the conduct of American foreign affairs under two Presidents who had no basic interest in matters outside the American borders. He had weathered and won in the stormy struggle that marked the revulsion of Americans against involvement in world affairs. His victories were not readily apparent, except that he built the foreign service of the United States into a strong and useful organization, after it had been nearly wrecked in the Wilson administration.

Successor to Secretary Hughes in this sensitive post in this period of vacuum in presidential power was Frank Billings Kellogg, who had been serving as American ambassador to Great Britain. Secretary Kellogg had also been a delegate to the Fifth Pan-American Conference in 1923 and had served a term as United States senator, during which he was a member of the Foreign Relations Committee. He came to office late in January, 1925, straight from Paris, where he had been working with Ambassador Myron Herrick on the negotiation of international agreement. Kellogg's unfortunate personality did much to keep the department in a state of constant unrest, and thus decreased its effectiveness as an instrument of foreign policy.

Kellogg was under constant critical scrutiny by the press, largely because he followed so impressive a figure, and many newspapers had supposed that Herbert Hoover would be the next Secretary of State. The Secretary's reaction to unfavorable criticism was to complain bitterly to his subordinates about their actions before sitting down to listen to their explanations. Consequently, his subordinates began to wince when

Frank Billings Kellogg

they read criticisms in the press, and to avoid criticism by any reasonable means, which included avoiding newspapermen. The press was quickly responsive to this attitude, and retaliated by an even more critical outlook on the department, so that matters did not improve at all.

The last half of the 1920's was marked by the emergence of a new attitude toward visitors to the United States, and it could be said that this was directly attributable to the relatively new problem posed by the international revolutionary activities of the Comintern, or Communist International Committee. Since the days of Thomas Jefferson and Citizen Genêt, the United States had generally granted foreign visitors the right to come into the country and speak as they pleased. The banning of travel as an instrument of national policy scarcely occurred to American governments, except in times of severe crisis when Americans might be forbidden to travel to disturbed areas, and citizens of nations warring with the United States were interned and otherwise restricted.

In the autumn of 1925, when the Interparliamentary Union planned to meet in Washington, a Communist member of the British House of Commons, named Shapurji Saklatvala, planned to attend. He was denied entrance into the United States because, Secretary Kellogg said, a speech Saklatvala made in Parliament indicated that he intended to carry on Communist propaganda in the United States. The next year Madame Alexandra Kollontai, a Soviet diplomat, was denied a transit visa to cross the United States to her post in Mexico because she was an "outstanding member of the Russian Communist party."

Nor was the denial of the right of travel in the United States restricted to Communists. The Countess Karolyi, the wife of former President of Hungary and a prominent lecturer, was denied permission to visit the United States. No

193

real reason was given, even though the matter went to the courts. Eventually it was revealed that the countess was denied entrance because members of the State Department were irritated at remarks made by the *Count* on a previous visit.

This high-handed attitude was manifest also in the State Department's attitudes toward other nations. Secretary Hughes and others had been mindful of the sad record of the United States in Latin America. Secretary Kellogg added to that record in an unprecedented statement about Mexican affairs in which he indicated that a new revolution might be brewing there. Mexican President Plutarco Calles was furious and said so. Relations between Mexico and the United States had been very cordial in 1924. Thereafter, during all of Secretary Kellogg's tenure, relations were most uncordial, and in 1927 they were very nearly broken off after the Secretary had made an irresponsible and unfriendly statement linking the Mexican government with Moscow. Knowing what he had done (the press informed him in no uncertain terms), Secretary Kellogg did take steps to make amends, and secured the appointment of businessman Dwight Morrow as ambassador. Morrow went to Mexico in 1927 as a friendly and reasonable man, and did manage to repair some of the damage.

Toward the end of the Coolidge administration a move came that showed the United States beginning to advance toward the center of the world stage again. In 1927, in a speech in the United States, French Foreign Minister Aristide Briand suggested a pact between the United States and France outlawing war as a means of settlement of international disputes. Senator William Borah, the isolationist leader, suggested that the idea be extended to all nations, and from this came a treaty called the Kellogg-Briand Pact, signed by 15 nations. Secretary Kellogg regarded this treaty as his greatest achievement, and it was the basis on which he became the first American Secretary of State to be awarded the Nobel Peace Prize (1929). His "achievement" lasted either two years or 10, depending on whether one considers the beginning of World War II to have been the march of the Japanese into Manchuria or the march of the Germans into Poland.

True internationalism, however, was achieved in the next administration, although since so many of President Herbert Hoover's policies were frustrated by the march of events his administration is not generally remembered in this capacity. Hoover's Secretary of State was Colonel Henry L. Stimson, a man of independent means who had served for many years in various capacities in government. He had been a United States Attorney, Secretary of War in the Taft cabinet, special emissary of President Coolidge to Nicaragua, and governor general of the Philippine Islands dependency. He was an administrator and a strong personality. How long he and President Hoover would get along seemed problematical, because Hoover was a strong President and one thoroughly versed in international affairs since his days as a mining engineer and international relief administrator at the end of World War I.

Those who looked for fireworks did not find them. The two men got along admirably, with far more of a partnership approach to their relationship then was usually the case with strong Presidents and vigorous Secretaries of State.

The Hoover administration believed in international participation, as became evident in the 25 new treaties of arbitration and 17 treaties of conciliation to which the United States agreed. The ban on travel of persons of unpopular views was reversed. Madame Karolyi received her passport. A militant pacifist, named Dorothy Detzer, was allowed to travel

195

Henry Lewis Stimson

abroad, although she refused to take the usual loyalty oath, under which one promised to bear arms in defense of the United States. Secretary Stimson and President Hoover even attempted to secure American adherence to the World Court of International Justice, although the Senate still would not accept such direct participation in world affairs because it meant a measure of potential control of national policy by outsiders.

The early days of the Hoover administration were days of hope and confidence that war could be outlawed and actually prevented, and the foreign policy aims of Hoover and his Secretary of State were aimed toward this end. War had been outlawed, theoretically, by the Kellogg-Briand Treaty. To decrease the physical danger, two areas needed exploration. One was the limitation of naval arms (since the results of the Washington Naval Conference had not been all that could be desired). A second area was that of land armament, where equally large amounts of money could be saved if agreement on limitation was reached.

Together, working as senior and junior partners, President Hoover and Secretary Stimson attacked the problem of naval disarmament, a puzzling one, because each nation used different methods of building, arming and measuring its warships. (To give a simplified example: How did one equate a ship with a dozen four-inch guns with one bearing eight six-inch guns.)

First, the Americans approached the British government to secure as much of a united front as was possible. Here it was discovered that while Prime Minister Ramsay MacDonald and President Hoover could arrive at a formula, the admirals of both nations vigorously opposed the whole proceeding and tried to frustrate control by giving misleading figures and estimates. Finally, Secretary Stimson laid down the law to the American admirals. He accused them of lying. They admitted "camouflaging," and he told them to stop it.

In January, 1930, the London Naval Conference was held. It failed, generally speaking, because the French would not compromise unless the United States would enter a general three-power defense pact in Europe, and Hoover and Stimson knew the United States Senate would never accept such a treaty. Still, some agreement on limitation was reached, particularly in regard to submarines.

The problem of limitation of land armaments seemed possible of solution. A World Disarmament Conference had been called by the League of Nations for 1932 at Geneva. Secretary Stimson was sufficiently hopeful for this meeting so that he traveled to Europe in the summer of 1931 for preliminary talks with European leaders and returned to Europe for the actual meeting. But Europe was not seriously ready to disarm in 1932, and America could not make the necessary gesture of guaranteeing American participation in European defense. The meeting was a failure.

In regard to Latin America, the United States was more restrained, more conciliatory, and more successful than it had been in earlier administrations. President Hoover spoke out against American intervention in Latin American affairs, and Secretary Stimson gave proof to the statement by securing the withdrawal of American marines from Nicaragua, where they had been stationed for so long. There were difficulties when Brazil's government was overthrown and the State Department imposed an arms embargo on both sides. The existing government claimed the United States had thus supported the rebels, but this policy would be justified and often repeated, and outcries against nonintervention went disregarded by most other Latin American nations.

The Wilsonian policy regarding recognition of nations became an embarrassment in Asia when Russia and China were engaged in hostilities, and Secretary Stimson rebuked Russia for not adhering to the Kellogg-Briand Treaty outlawing war. The Russians angrily reminded the United States that it was interfering in their affairs without any justification, since, as far as America was concerned, Soviet Russia did not exist.

But the end of the Kellogg-Briand Treaty was in sight with the Japanese invasion of China in 1931. In this matter, the President and his Secretary of State showed their one known disagreement on matters of basic policy. Stimson wanted to take strong action against Japan. The President said the United States must show its disapproval of Japanese aggression only through economic sanctions and nonrecognition of Japanese conquests. This policy came to be known as the Hoover-Stimson Doctrine. The Secretary was soon convinced of its propriety and supported it fully. It failed because European nations were slow in joining any massive attempt to boycott or surround Japan with sanctions, and because Japan was determined to expand into Chinese territory. Only Secretary Stimson's original idea of using extreme measures, in connection with other nations, might have restrained the Japanese. President Hoover could not be convinced that military measures should be used, but even had he been convinced, the other nations involved, Britain and France in particular, would never have agreed to such action at that time. Historically, it may seem easy to pinpoint the place where policy went wrong, but it must be remembered that the United States was totally dedicated to the principles of the Kellogg-Briand Treaty outlawing war.

During most of the Hoover administration, the United States and Europe were suffering from a serious economic depression, and this dislocation exerted considerable influence on foreign relations. After world markets collapsed in

1929, the President authorized a moratorium on war debts to the United States, and Secretary Stimson suggested an international monetary conference. While the idea was being worked out among the nations, the American presidential elections were held, and the internationally minded Republican administration was defeated. So the next steps in American foreign relations would be taken by a new administration, that of Franklin Delano Roosevelt. To sum up the idealism and internationalism with which Secretary Stimson looked upon his world, one might cite his destruction of the famous Black Chamber, or code-breaking office of the State Department, which had been in operation for more than 15 years. The office had been very successful in breaking diplomatic and other codes used by various nations. But when Secretary Stimson came to office he disbanded the code-breaking section of the department on the grounds that gentlemen did not read each other's mail. So great was the faith of the Stimson Secretariat in the dignity and goodness of mankind.

From Isolation to War

Although one does not usually consider Franklin Delano Roosevelt in the role of isolationist, there was a definite element of isolationism in the Roosevelt administration in its earliest days. It was probably brought about by an overwhelming concern over serious domestic problems, a concern so great that President Roosevelt chose a tax expert as his Secretary of State.

Senator Cordell Hull, who took the appointment with some reluctance, was largely known as the principal sponsor of the federal income tax law, and he declared himself that he was interested in foreign affairs largely because of his opposition to the high protective tariff policy generally espoused by the Republicans. Yet Hull was not isolationist by nature. At least he had supported President Wilson's fight for the League of Nations.

Franklin Roosevelt was determined to be his own Secretary of State, and Secretary Hull was to be his trusted adviser. Hull understood his position, and, generally speaking, functioned well in it. He advised, and although his advice was often ignored, he maintained good temper and returned to advise again.

President Roosevelt was intensely political by nature, and many of his appointments to State Department positions were made for political purposes. He chose Professor Raymond Moley of Columbia University to be Assistant Secretary of State, although Moley had no real bent for foreign policy, and he and Hull could never get along. His reason for selecting Moley was to give him a prominent position in which Moley might continue as adviser and speech writer, roles he had played in the "brain trust" of the political campaign. But Moley took his position as Secretary seriously, and his downfall came with the London Economic Conference, arranged by President Hoover and Secretary Stimson.

President Roosevelt began his exercise of foreign-policy-making by approving the Hoover-Stimson Doctrine on China. His second move concerned the London Conference, finally known as the World Economic and Financial Conference. This meeting was held in London in the summer of 1933, and Secretary Hull went there with a number of delegates. But since President Roosevelt had chosen the delegates himself, they represented several different points of view, from that of isolationist Senator James Couzens to that of internationalist James M. Cox, Democratic presidential candidate of 1920, to those of a group of New Dealers including the ultraliberal Rexford G. Tugwell.

Secretary Hull went to London expecting support for his plan to arrange reciprocal trade agreements and cut tariff barriers. Before Hull reached London, President Roosevelt had changed his mind. Roosevelt sent Assistant Secretary of State Raymond Moley to London bearing recommendations about stabilization of currencies. However, before Moley ar-

Cordell Hull

rived in London, President Roosevelt had changed his mind again.

Finally, as these Americans of so many different political bents schemed among themselves and talked with other delegates, the President repudiated all he had said to any of them by a unique and unsupportable message to the conference. Delegates from the other nations were ready to call for immediate adjournment and name the United States as responsible for the failure of the conference. Only the diplomacy of Secretary Hull prevented this indignity from being heaped on the United States. But whatever else had happened, American economic influence in Europe was, for the time being, lost completely, as was foreign respect for the new administration.

President Roosevelt actually did not much care. His concern was the American home front. As far as foreign affairs were concerned, he concentrated, as did Secretary Hull, on the development of a Good Neighbor Policy in Latin America, and was more concerned with this policy than anyone since the days of James G. Blaine. At a conference in Montevideo, for the first time, the United States persuaded other American delegations to take the lead in guiding hemispheric relations, and thus increased American prestige to a level hitherto unmatched. President Roosevelt himself went to Buenos Aires to attend an extraordinary Inter-American Conference, and, although it was not successful in setting up machinery for keeping the peace, the idea was planted there and began to grow.

Secretary Hull wanted to eliminate the awkward recognition policy that the Wilson administration had bequeathed to the United States, and he brought up with the President the question of American recognition of the government of the Soviet Union. Roosevelt agreed, and he conducted the negotiations with Maxim Litvinov, foreign minister and the special representative of the President of the Russian government.

In the negotiations, attempts were made to settle old debts of the Russian state to America and Americans, and to eliminate Soviet revolutionary propaganda in the United States. But the Russians, who had not trusted the United States since the abortive Siberian adventure of 1919–1920, broke their promises, and continued to promote international revolution, including Communist revolution in the United States. Thus the Russians perpetuated the basis for distrust in America that was to bear its evil fruit in the 40's, 50's, and 60's, and to threaten world peace. Whether or not a different American attitude during the years from 1917 to 1933 would have made any difference was a matter that would be long and uselessly debated.

Throughout the years, there had been various reorganizations of the Department of State to create efficiency, to cut down costs and to expand activities. Most notable of these was the establishment of a Division of Cultural Relations in the department, which broadened the department's sphere of activity enormously. It came during the second Roosevelt administration, with Secretary Hull continuing in office.

Congress, in the middle 1930's, was far more isolationist than was the administration. Secretary Hull was disturbed by a congressional move to enforce strict American neutrality through an embargo on shipments of arms and other war materials. Hull's position did not carry, although President Roosevelt supported him. The isolationists, led by Senator Borah, were too powerful. They were impelled to action by seeing the eruption of wars in Ethiopia, Manchuria, China and Spain. They believed, erroneously, that the United States could remain neutral in a world struggle.

By the late 1930's, Secretary Hull was dubious about the efficacy of any attempts by the United States government to maintain world peace. The hopes that had been so high during the Hoover years were dashed to pieces. Some State Department officials believed that personal appeals by President Roosevelt to Hitler, Mussolini and other European leaders might change the course of history, but Hull did not. He cooperated with the President in trying to create a climate of acceptance and worked on the texts of the messages, but they accomplished absolutely nothing. Hitler and Mussolini rejected the private appeals in public addresses to their followers.

Secretary Hull sometimes exerted a decisive influence on American policy, as in the matter of continued Japanese expansion. He had seen Japan moving and he viewed her moves with great suspicion. In the summer of 1939, he wrote the Japanese ambassador, telling him that the United States wished to terminate the treaty of commerce and navigation that had existed between the two nations since 1911. Secretary Hull wasted no words in telling the Japanese that their actions were creating hostility in America. On another occasion, he encouraged Ambassador Joseph Grew, back from Japan, to make a strong speech to the American-Japan Society against Japanese aggression.

In 1914, the diplomatic representatives of America in Europe were almost all surprised by the outbreak of war, weeks after the assassination at Sarajevo. Not so in 1939—the American diplomatic corps abroad was fully conscious of the international situation, and warned that Hitler would attack, warned that he would attack Poland, and gave the approximate time. Secretary Hull was in his office, and was conferring with his assistants long before the British government in London even knew there had been an invasion. The

State Department had come along way in a quarter of a century in its methods of operation.

With the outbreak of war in Europe, the United States proclaimed its neutrality. But it was not the same kind of neutrality that occurred in the beginning of World War I. President Roosevelt took matters into his own hands and sent Undersecretary of State Sumner Welles on a mission to Europe to see if there was any chance of making peace. Unfortunately, the President did not discuss this move with Secretary Hull before acting, and consequently Hull was opposed to the idea. Soon, Hull and Welles were not getting along, and the unity of the State Department was shattered. One reason for this was the growing interest of President Roosevelt in the field of foreign relations, and his acting without consulting the Secretary of State, much in the Wilsonian manner. When the Germans marched into Paris and the French government fled, Ambassador Bullitt was in Paris, reporting directly to President Roosevelt, and Secretary Hull appointed his own ambassador, Anthony Biddle, to represent the United States to the fleeing French government. To say that American policy was confusing was to put it mildly.

The major problem of the State Department after passage of a neutrality act in November, 1939, was to give a semblance of neutrality to a government which was very much unneutral. President Roosevelt felt the need to remain neutral, but his emotions were all the other way. Congress was not ready for intervention, nor were a great many of the American people, but the people who knew what was happening in the world—the diplomats—were very much inclined toward intervention against the totalitarian governments before it was too late to be effective and save any of Europe.

In 1940, the State Department superintended the exchange of 50 ancient American destroyers for eight British naval and air bases which could be used to protect the Western Hemisphere. This was an unneutral transaction, and it caused the department considerable pain in determining how to go about it with the least danger of being accused of an outright breach of international law. The problem was to satisfy American public opinion; no attempt was made nor was needed to try to persuade the Axis powers where American sympathies lay. Secretary Hull was hard put to keep his diplomats from speaking their minds objectively, and several of them had to be recalled "for consultation" after particularly inflammatory speeches about America's need to prepare for war.

In spite of the great growth of the United States, in 1940, the State Department numbered fewer than a thousand employees. This was not much of an increase from the 750, or so, of the early 1920's, considering the change in the nation and the growth of federal government during the depression years. With the war in Europe and the movement of Americans to bases in the Western Hemisphere, new problems were created. With the complications of war, President Roosevelt continued to use "special emissaries" who reported to him and not to the Department of State, to the growing annoyance of Secretary Hull. Particularly after the beginning of 1941, Mr. Roosevelt began to conduct personal diplomacy. For example, in August that year, he took Acting Secretary Sumner Welles to a meeting place in a Newfoundland harbor, and there, with Winston Churchill, produced the Atlantic Charter. Secretary Hull was recuperating from an illness at White Sulphur Springs at the time, and he knew very little about the entire affair. Roosevelt maintained a disturbing habit of communicating directly with heads of state when he felt like it. He sent personal letters to Marshal Pétain and to

Premier Stalin. He made a personal protest to the Japanese ambassador, Baron Nomura, when the Japanese moved into Indochina in July, 1941, and he personally ordered the freezing of Japanese assets in the United States, a few days later.

And yet President Roosevelt did not interfere as much in the general aspects of foreign-policy management as this all might indicate. Hull saw Nomura scores of times, with and without the President. Sometimes it has been suggested that the United States could have avoided war with Japan by more expert diplomacy. Secretary Hull has been accused of forcing the Japanese into war by an ultimatum issued late in November, 1941. But the fact is that Japan had long since decided on war with the United States, and when the negotiations reached the November stage, the time and place of the attack had already been determined and the task force was nearly ready to depart.

By the first of December, Secretary Hull stated that diplomacy had run its course, had failed, and that the next step was up to the military and naval defenders of America. He warned that a surprise attack might be expected momentarily. Then came the attack on Pearl Harbor, and the Department of State prepared to do what it could do in war.

The greatest mistake made by President Roosevelt in World War II was his decision not to use the State Department in the war. As Commander in Chief he dealt directly with the military commanders on war matters, often leaving Secretary Hull in ignorance of actions and plans. This proved disastrous in the peace that followed the war, for the world had changed too much by the 1940's to separate diplomacy from military force.

The State Department was kept busy during the war, however, even when not consulted on the highest levels of policy. One of its tasks was to work out a declaration of principles

Edward Stettinius

of the anti-Axis states (which became the United Nations) professing common war aims. Another task was to persuade the Latin American nations to break off diplomatic relations with the Axis. Sumner Welles handled this program at the Rio de Janeiro conference, with Secretary Hull remaining in Washington and issuing general instructions. Welles exceeded his instructions and Hull reprimanded him. But President Roosevelt sided with Welles, whereupon the Secretary of State left the department for several months to "recuperate from illness." Secretary Hull did come back, however. President Roosevelt needed him and he had a way of persuading men he needed.

The war brought enlargements to the State Department, with the increase in functions, and by the end of 1942 some 2,500 persons were employed in various divisions. Among the many problems in which the State Department participated was relief for people in areas captured from the Axis powers. This problem was complicated by military- and foreign-policy conflicts, plus the policies of the Office of Foreign Relief and Rehabilitation, which was nominally responsible to the State Department. Such planning could only make for friction, and it came. In addition, the friction between Secretary Hull and Undersecretary Welles grew so strong that in the fall of 1943 Welles resigned. He was replaced by Edward R. Stettinius, Jr., a businessman who knew nothing about the State Department. Secretary Hull had rid himself of his most piercing thorn, but he had acquired a new one, nearly as sharp and rasping. There was little friction between the two men but only because Cordell Hull's health began to fail. In November, 1944, he resigned after nearly 12 years of service.

When President Roosevelt announced the appointment of Stettinius as Secretary of State, Washingtonians harked back to the days of President Wilson. It was apparent that the

President intended to be his own Secretary of State. Stettinius had already reorganized the State Department to attempt to put it on a "business" basis. He reorganized it again in December, 1944. A change was necessary, for the department consisted of 3,700 employees, plus 7,000 members of the foreign service, and the administrative machinery was creaking.

Edward Stettinius was Secretary for seven months, from the end of November, 1944, to the end of June, 1945, and during that period he spent more than half his time attending international conferences abroad, dealing with the war and the peace. He increased the staff of the Secretary from 70 to 130, and went to one international conference with a delegation of 79 persons. (The Mexican government, the host, used only 41 persons.)

The Stettinius term of office was noteworthy for a new, or almost new, attempt to secure a change in tradition in the administration of American foreign policy. In 1944, the idea of a permanent organization to enforce international security was brought up, and a conference was scheduled for Dumbarton Oaks, an estate in Georgetown. Stettinius headed the American delegation to Dumbarton Oaks, from which came the seeds of the United Nations Organization. Earlier, Stettinius and Secretary Hull had been responsible for the attempt to develop a bi-partisan foreign policy. Hull had become concerned about harsh words spoken by Republican presidential candidate Thomas E. Dewey, and Dewey was invited to send a representative to discuss foreign policy. John Foster Dulles was sent, and Hull worked out an agreement with him to guard against the placement of the postwar world under great power domination, as the Republicans said they feared the Democrats were doing. Stettinius continued this policy, and often called Dulles and other prominent

Republican leaders to various conferences as advisers and consultants.

Secretary Stettinius was also noteworthy because he carried through the San Francisco Conference, at which the United Nations was born. By this time, President Roosevelt had died, and President Harry Truman had taken office. Stettinius was ready to resign, but, as the conference was pending, Truman asked Stettinius to carry on until it was finished. On June 27, 1945, the day after the 50 nations at the conference signed the United Nations Charter, Secretary Stettinius resigned. The United States was approaching a new era in foreign policy.

The Cold War

There was a lesson to be learned from the tendency of strong Presidents to avoid the increasingly cumbersome machinery of diplomacy and seek settlement of problems by personal negotiation—and the lesson came home to the United States almost as soon as World War II had ended.

President Roosevelt had trusted many personal envoys. He had often sent Harry Hopkins, a personal assistant, to talk to leaders of other states. Vice-President Henry Wallace sometimes went abroad, too, on friendship missions, and so did many others, even including Eric Johnston, president of the United States Chamber of Commerce.

There was absolutely nothing wrong in such missions, as long as they did not interfere with the orderly processes of diplomacy. In this regard, Henry Hopkins was a Secretary of State's dream, because he never interfered. Henry Wallace was a nightmare, because he interfered enormously. But even such interferences could be coped with, and were not the major problem. The real disservice to the nation rendered by personal diplomacy in World War II was in the atmosphere it created.

No matter what they said and did across the caviar and vodka, the leaders of the Soviet Union never deviated from their initial aims. To them, the war against Germany and Japan was simply a phase of a total war. According to their long-range plan, they were out to revolutionize the world. Their short-range plan was to encircle themselves with nations governed by Communists, whom they could control.

Premier Stalin knew this when he went to the vital meeting at Yalta, in the Crimea, with Prime Minister Churchill and President Roosevelt. The latter, in particular, was most unsuspecting, gulled by his own advisers. Nor was it that the State Department did not know what to expect. The State Department had never been better informed; Ambassador Averell Harriman and Soviet affairs expert George Kennan had both warned what would happen. Others in the department were equally aware of the dangers. They spoke of them freely, but the White House was not listening.

There was nothing wrong with the agreements reached at Yalta, providing for joint occupations, creation of "broadly representative governments" in Europe and elsewhere, except that within a month Russia was repudiating every one of them and Prime Minister Churchill and President Roosevelt knew it. But this was on the eve of the President's death, the war was practically over, and there was little that could be done.

Harry Truman came to the presidency in April, 1945, saddled with a Department of State in the throes of reorganization, headed by Secretary of State Stettinius, who had neither the aptitude nor the training for the job, and an overwhelming national desire to find peace. So President Truman continued the Roosevelt policy of collaboration with the Russians, see-

James Francis Byrnes

ing them put their foot in many more doors, dividing Germany and Austria and giving Russia new territory. All this happened at Potsdam in July, 1945. The new Secretary of State, James F. Byrnes, had been in office less than a month. He had a long government history as congressman, United States senator, Supreme Court justice, and "Assistant President"; and he had been at Yalta. He was an internationalist and a shrewd political leader, too, although not a professional diplomat.

A period began that was to last for many years, a period in which the Secretary of State began to function as a sort of supreme ambassador. Secretary Byrnes went to Potsdam. Within a month he was back in Europe attending a foreign ministers' meeting. Then, however, Secretary Byrnes came back to get down to business, which meant a reorganization of the Department of State to meet new problems.

During the war, the Office of War Information had been established, largely to distribute American propaganda abroad. This function was taken over by the Department of State late in 1945. So was part of the intelligence function carried out in wartime by the Office of Strategic Services. Another portion of the Office of Strategic Services work was transferred to a new agency, called the Central Intelligence Agency.

Before World War II, it might have seemed unlikely to Americans that an espionage agency would be an integral part of America's dealings with other nations. Less than 20 years earlier, Secretary Stimson had remarked, "Gentlemen do not read each other's mail." But in the postwar world there was no place for such gentlemen—if any were left. Every nation was doing its utmost to read one another's mail. The nations could be divided into two groups: the Western World and the Communist World. The Central Intelligence Agency and its function became essential to the conduct of the new kind of diplomacy, even though it did present problems that were entirely unfamiliar to the members of an open society. A secret intelligence agency is a frightening and sometimes frightful thing in a democratic republic, and the problem from the beginning was to harness the potentially dangerous agency as a useful servant.

Between July, 1945, and the beginning of 1947, Secretary Byrnes spent more time in foreign capitals than he did in Washington. The State Department then was run by Undersecretary Dean Acheson. He was in charge at home during the 18 months when the bitter fruits of American trustfulness were harvested. He bore much of the brunt of congressional and public disapproval of events that followed policies laid down by the highest authority during the wartime years. The Secretary could be compared to a fireman, who spent his entire term in office running from one national capital to another, putting out fires that had been lit before he came to power. Byrnes had more power in the conduct of American foreign relations than any other Secretary since Charles Evans Hughes. But his role was a negative one of trying to piece together a torn world, struggling against the constant incursions of the Soviet Union. Had the Department of State not been filled with strong and knowledgeable men in 1945 and 1946, the situation that faced America at the beginning of 1947 might have been much worse than it was. As has been indicated, a succession of Secretaries of State, beginning with Charles Evans Hughes, had worked hard trying to build up the professional character of the United States foreign service.

In December, 1946, Secretary Byrnes resigned, to be replaced by General George C. Marshall, special presidential aide to China and former chief of staff of the United States

George C. Marshall

army during World War II. His appointment was well received by press and public; it was also indicative of a trend in American thinking. Suddenly Americans realized the war was not over; it seemed entirely proper to select as Secretary of State a military man who had directed the army in the war and who had accompanied Presidents Roosevelt and Truman to all the major wartime conferences of heads of state. Secretary Marshall was more familiar with the world situation on a higher level than any other man in America.

Even before the end of the war, the United States had been busy with relief, which was a movement more than a program. The movement represented American thinking that the best way to bring peace was to make help available to the victims of war. One program was the United Nations Relief and Rehabilitation Administration, which spent about a billion dollars a year, with the United States putting up 68 percent of the money. A World Bank had been set up to help needy nations. Trade restrictions were reduced sharply.

Yet, early in the Secretaryship of General Marshall, it became apparent that these programs were not enough; nor was it enough to adopt a hardening American line toward Soviet excesses at the conference table. In spite of a fairly large segment of American opinion which believed that the United States policy toward Russia was too harsh, compromise with the Russians was leading only to disaster everywhere. In the spring of 1947, the British government informed Washington that Britain would have to withdraw its troops that were in occupation of Greece, maintaining order after the Nazi occupation. The British were in Greece in 1947 because, two years after the war, Communist guerrilla forces still threatened to take control of the country, and King George V of Greece asked them to remain. At the same time, Turkey was threatened by economic collapse and So-

220

viet incursions along her northern border.

When the British news reached the White House, President Truman acted swiftly on his own. He decided to pick up the British commitments, and in so doing he enunciated the Truman Doctrine, which was "to support freed peoples who are resisting attempted subjugation by armed minorities or by outside pressures."

The Truman Doctrine represented the first major positive move in American foreign policy since the end of World War II. It was a considered attempt to contain the Soviet Union, and it was quickly recognized as a master stroke. This doctrine was followed by the Marshall Plan, suggested by Secretary Marshall in a 1947 commencement address at Harvard College. The Marshall Plan called for European nations to organize master plans for their own reconstruction. The United States would then furnish the funds and equipment to start the plans working.

To show that this was an open attempt to achieve peace and prosperity, Russia and the Communist world were invited to join in this program, but they refused, apparently afraid of the eroding quality of open contact with the Western World.

Thus, President Truman stepped in among those strong Presidents who managed foreign relations themselves. But such were Secretary Marshall's qualities that there was no friction between President and Secretary of State. Truman called his secretary "the greatest living American" and invariably followed Marshall's advice when it was given. The Secretary, in turn, was completely loyal to the President. Perhaps part of this can be explained by Marshall's long military training. But part of it was due to his personal respect for the presidency, and another part might have been due to Marshall's absence of personal ambition for the presidency.

Steadily, after 1947, the United States moved afield in its exercise of a vigorous foreign policy. It was hoped that the United Nations might become the central agency for settlement of all international disputes. However, the organization of the United Nations was such that any major power on the Security Council could present quick, positive action to keep the peace. Some American faith in the United Nations was lost during the Palestine crisis of 1948, when a new state of Israel was created in such a manner that it must be a constant source of friction.

The United States, through the partnership of President Truman and Secretary Marshall, moved to create a separate force for security of the West—the North Atlantic Treaty of April, 1949, which set up a joint military command of all participating nations.

This step represented a diplomatic and military victory for the West—one might call it diplo-military—for after 1947 it seemed there could be no separation of diplomacy from immediate threat of force. The world had become an open cockpit where power and power alone counted, and where such diplomatic terms as *détente* and *démarche* no longer carried serious meaning. But containment of Communism in the West was followed by a Communist outbreak in Asia in 1949. After four years of struggle, the Chinese Communists overcame the weak and corrupt Nationalist government, and the Far East trembled as with the coming of a major storm.

Secretary Marshall resigned in January, 1949, because of ill health. He and President Truman enjoyed what has been called a perfect partnership. Marshall was succeeded by Dean Acheson, who had served the State Department as Assistant Secretary and Undersecretary, and who had resigned earlier for financial reasons to return to private law practice.

222

Dean Acheson

Secretary Acheson served for four years, and to him they must have seemed the longest years in his life, for during all of them the Department of State was under constant congressional fire because of the failure of the American government to stop world communism dead in its tracks. Partly the attack was political. Dean Acheson came to symbolize American foreign policy, and the Republicans saw in foreign policy the weak point they could attack in the presidential election campaign of 1952. But there were other considerations than political. One was pure frustration of those who wished to see communism destroyed or contained. Another was resentment against American initiative and American support of the United Nations war against Communist aggression in Korea. The Korean War began in 1950, and two years later it was most unpopular because it was not won. And so the Secretary of State became the symbol of America's failure to return to a "normalcy" which would let the United States relax and bask in prosperity.

The congressional attacks on the State Department had one serious effect on American foreign policy that cannot be underestimated. These attacks drove some of the finest professional foreign-service officers from the government, among them experts on the Far East and Russia, in particular. Perhaps even worse than this effect was the very definite cowing of the remaining members of the department. President Truman was never cowed about his foreign policy nor was Dean Acheson, but because of the flood of loyalty investigations and charges of Communist influence, many State Department officers felt it much wiser to refrain from stating unpopular views, even in confidential conversations and documents.

In the quarter century following the beginning of World War II, there occurred more activity in the field of American foreign relations than in all the years of the American republic preceding that time, because the United States had become one of the two most powerful nations of the world and was the leading nation of the West. Thus, the President and the Secretary of State were faced with almost daily crises in foreign affairs. But while these crises were handled with considerable skill in the Truman period, the same cannot be said for the Eisenhower administrations, when John Foster Dulles became Secretary of State.

Dulles had spent his entire life planning to become Secretary of State. His grandfather, John Foster, had held the office, and members of the family had served in other high positions.

Dulles became the most powerful of all Secretaries of State in history, because he served under a weak President, who acceded to all that he suggested. Under Dulles came the formation of the Southeast Asia Treaty Organization, which was to involve the United States in the Vietnam war; the nations signing agreed to defend one another against attack. Between 1953 and 1956, Secretary Dulles so mishandled Middle Eastern relationships that President Nasser of Egypt, believing that he had American support, closed the Suez Canal, and threatened Israel so that she attacked. Britain and France tried to interfere in the time-honored fashion of big powers, but the United States refused to help, and the British and French were forced to withdraw in the face of world opinion. Out of this fiasco came the seeds of a breach in the North Atlantic Treaty Organization alliance (France was furious and the French thereafter distrusted the United States), contempt for the United States in the Middle Eastern world, and failure for the United Nations.

That same year, 1956, a revolution broke out in Hungary, a country to which the unofficial American Radio Free

John Foster Dulles

Europe had been broadcasting hopefully. Secretary Dulles and other Republicans had spoken of the "liberation of captive nations" in the election campaign of 1952, and some Hungarians believed them. But when the chips were down, America did nothing.

So it went, with force being applied in the Middle East again during an attack on Lebanon, threats of force everywhere, and a growing distrust by America's allies of her intentions and reliability.

For the purposes of this study of the Secretary of State and the pattern of American foreign policy, it is impossible to consider every foreign policy decision of Secretary Dulles. Nor is it necessary to consider all the decisions. What was unique about the Dulles' Secretaryship was the immense power he wielded and the tiny respect he secured for it. Even within the Department of State there was fretting and weakening, because Dulles consistently undermined his ambassadors and ignored his advisers.

Latin America was the arena for another American fiasco. In 1954, the United States became concerned because Jacob Arbenz, the dictator of Guatemala, seemed to be putting his country into the hands of the Communists. Using a resolution of the Organization of American States, the United States government armed Guatemalan exiles and helped them to oust their government. This intervention created a strong anti-Americanism throughout Latin America, so strong that when Vice-President Nixon later toured Latin America he was stoned, and President Eisenhower threatened to send the marines into Venezuela to protect him.

American foreign policy had moved far away from the days when "Gentlemen do not open one another's mail," and there was no greater proof of it than the infamous U-2 incident of 1959.

Christian Herter

For some years, the United States had been sending high altitude photographic observation planes over Communist countries to take pictures of various installations. In September, 1959, the Russians shot down one such plane over Russian territory. When the Soviets announced this fact, the White House denied it, then President Eisenhower admitted it. No one knew what to believe, and Premier Khrushchev used the incident to discredit the United States and to break off talks about a new "summit conference" of leaders of the world.

Two new developments vital to foreign policy were indicated in that last paragraph. The first was the practice of espionage, which had become the normal work of the Central Intelligence Agency. The second one was the "summit meeting" idea, which had come to dominate the world of diplomacy. No longer were ambassadors "plenipotentiary and extraordinary"; through the summit meeting the ambassadors were reduced to intermediaries. Some critics of Secretary Dulles said that by his insistence on carrying on all negotiations himself on every subject, he had made office boys of his ambassadors.

The U-2 incident, however, could not be blamed on Secretary Dulles. He had resigned, plagued by ill health, and Christian Herter had become Eisenhower's second Secretary of State. Secretary Herter came to office in the spring of 1959, and affairs began to quiet down a bit in the Department of State.

There was one further fiasco, which could not be laid at Secretary Herter's feet, either. It was the emergence of Fidel Castro's unique Marxist dictatorship of Cuba, which threatened to put an end to the Monroe Doctrine once and for all.

Summing up the failures of the Eisenhower administration in foreign policy, some critics called it "brinkmanship,"

Dean Rusk

which, they said, was the art of going to the brink of war without ever doing anything positive to save the situation. The trouble was that neither Eisenhower nor Dulles was sufficiently powerful or resolute or intelligent enough to meet the many American commitments without overstatement when the showdowns came.

The Eisenhower administration's conduct of foreign policy indicated the new complications of a nuclear world, but the real change in the American method of making foreign policy was to be indicated in three situations that developed in the following years, when Dean Rusk became Secretary of State.

The first problem came in April, 1961, when a force of 1,500 Cubans, trained with the help of the Central Intelligence Agency, launched an attack on Cuba. The Cubans believed they would have air support from the United States, but when the invading force reached the Bay of Pigs, President Kennedy refused to let the air force go in to protect them and the force was overwhelmed. In this difficulty, President Kennedy was advised by his Secretary of State, his Secretary of Defense, and his Central Intelligence Agency chief. He made the decision, which was a combination military-policy and foreign-policy decision.

The second problem came in the autumn of 1962, when the Russians, who believed the Kennedy administration to be as vacillating as the Eisenhower administration, sent missiles into Cuba. But guided by his Secretary of State, Secretary of Defense, and Central Intelligence Agency chief, the President on television exposed to the world U-2 photographs of the missile installations and said such provocation could not be accepted by the United States. Mobilization of American forces began. The gauntlet was cast down, telling Russia that the United States was ready to invade Cuba, and warning that if Russia came in to defend Cuba, a nuclear war might result.

Premier Khrushchev presumably consulted his own experts and decided to withdraw the missiles if the United States would not attack Cuba. It was agreed. The missiles went, and war did not come.

The third problem came in the late spring of 1967, when after much Arab saber rattling, the Israelis attacked their Arab neighbors. War in the Middle East seemed inevitable. With Russian ships and American ships in the Mediterranean, with Russian commitments to the Arabs and American sympathy for Israel, the situation might very well have developed into a world war again. This time, when the President heard the news in the middle of the night, he called into consultation his Secretary of State, his Secretary of Defense and his Central Intelligence Agency chief. Plans were made and in the next few days policies were enunciated, making it apparent that a new care was being exercised. The Israeli victory of July, 1967, brought new problems for American policy—not the least of which was the desertion of an American guarantee of the territorial integrity of all Middle Eastern nations. The guarantee had been made earlier to protect Israel, which demonstrated its ability to defend itself having won the war in 1967. But the American policy was outmoded, and there was difficulty in finding another that would not destroy United States prestige in the entire Moslem world.

Here was a great change, apparent in so many ways. Foreign policy no longer existed apart from military policy. Foreign policy could not await the normal diplomatic channels of information but must be decided on the immediate basis of information collected by intelligence agents. There was no time for studious approach or delay in this instant world of the 1960's. The Department of State had become a huge institution, with 111 embassies, two legations, and 180 other posts. It employed 7,500 Americans at home and 7,500 abroad (yet was still second smallest of the executive departments). The department consisted of the Secretary, two Undersecretaries with two deputies, a Policy Planning Council, with the Counselor of the Department as chairman, two Ambassadors-at-large who worked as troubleshooters, 11 bureaus and a half dozen smaller agencies.

With all this work force, the basic problems of foreign policy were still sufficiently unchanged so that the hands of dozens of previous Secretaries of State could be seen in the actions of the United States government in the 1960's. The Castro affair was controlled in part by the Monroe Doctrine of so many years earlier, and the Wilson doctrine of nonrecognition was still in force in regard to Communist China.

Above all, one change was apparently becoming more urgent in the years since the Roosevelt administration. It was no longer possible for a President to be his own Secretary of State, for the Secretary no longer had the degree of latitude and responsibility that could make him the chief adviser to the President. The National Security Council, which consisted of the leading officials in defense and foreign affairs posts, had replaced the Secretary as chief adviser. Government had become too large for it to be otherwise. The importance of the foreign relations function had increased immeasurably, and the importance of the Secretary of State had seriously declined.

The Colossus Years

As of the end of World War II, the world was divided into two basic blocs of nations: those that found themselves in the Soviet sphere of influence and those that found themselves, or chose to put themselves, in the American sphere of influence. And yet, even from the last days of the war, a third influence was at work, the formation of what the French, in their internal politics, called *"troisième force,"* and which came to be known as the Third World.

This Third World consisted, for the most part, of emerging nations in Latin America, Africa and the Far East. Not all the Third World agreed among itself: African nations quarreled, and so did Asiatics and Latin Americans. They had some odd heroes, for one, Sukarno of Indonesia. In a way, Marshall Tito of Yugoslavia was a stabilizing force.

American policy toward the Third World was slow to develop. For a time, there was a scurry to aid the Africans and the Latins. The Third World found its voice in the General Assembly of the United Nations, where the veto of the big powers did not count, and used it as a speaker's platform for the little nations of the world.

The emergence of the Third World was accompanied by an erosion of big-power world policy, and by the 1970's the old balance of power no longer counted for so much as it once had. Each emerging African nation demanded a new attention from the Department of State. The desks and sections dealing with Africa demanded new studies, and men of new and broader vision. Among other things, more opportunity had to be created in the State Department for black Americans.

The United States often found itself in difficult positions because the Third World was so varied in nature. A policy that would appeal to a Sukarno would not appeal to a Kwame Nkrumah. Then there was the problem of the emerging Arab world, where the United States had trouble trying to achieve some solidarity with Arabs, while maintaining its long history of friendship and sympathy with the Israelis, whom the Arabs considered their mortal enemies.

There is no better example of the continuity and complexity of American foreign policy in the last half of the twentieth century than in Vietnam, an area with which the author has been familiar since the Japanese surrender in 1945, when he spent several weeks in Hanoi and watched the unfolding of Ho Chi Minh's revolution.

In the latter part of the 1960's the problem of Vietnam dominated foreign policy. It also dominated defense policy and the whole American attitude. The fact that the policy was in hot debate at home, that the question of disengagement from Vietnam was at issue every day, underlined the dilemma in which American policy makers found themselves with regard to the complex world of the time.

At this point in history, almost every statement about Vietnam can be challenged. But every writer on the subject must make certain decisions and take certain positions and every government must do the same. One could say that, until 1954, the United States had no policy toward Vietnam, a fact that Ho Chi Minh resented bitterly. He felt that the American policy of the Atlantic Charter, the self-determination of peoples, would and should be followed at the end of World War II. But Ho was an old member of the Comintern, and, as such, his revolution was regarded by the Americans from the outset as sponsored by international communism and thus bound to end up part and parcel with the Communist states. Even in the 1950's, the United States position on communism and Communist governments was that they constituted a single force; the break between Moscow and Peking had not yet begun to seem important to Americans. Indeed even in the 1970's, American policy was still based on the unity of communism, even though the facts indicated that communism was as fragmented as the old capitalism had become at the end of World War II.

In 1954, at the end of a long and bloody war in Indochina, the French government was morally and economically exhausted. At Geneva that summer, agreements were made for the French and Vietminh forces of Ho Chi Minh to stop fighting and live under an armed truce. This was the international policy.

President Eisenhower did not press for the signing of the Geneva agreements by the United States. In a way, this was a hands-off policy. Yet, quietly, the American government began to give assistance to the French and Southern Vietnamese, whose government was established by the French. Actually, such assistance had begun under the Truman administration; it was increased under Eisenhower. The underlying aim of American foreign policy was to prevent

Communist domination where it could, for in the Truman days and thereafter, Communist domination was regarded as monolithic. In his memoirs, *Present at the Creation,* writing of a 1949 meeting with French foreign Minister Schuman in which the subject of Vietnam came up, Acheson said, "We believed that France could help more in preventing Communist domination by moving quickly to satisfy nationalist aspirations."

And elsewhere in his memoirs, Acheson indicated that American policy toward the old Indochina was a hodge-podge, that, even before the end of the Truman administration, bright heads in the State Department feared that America would become bogged down in Indochina.

The Geneva agreements had called for reunification of the old Indochina, or most of it, in two years. But the Communists of the North and the West-oriented government of the South could agree no more than could the opposites in Korea or in Germany. The idea was doomed to failure.

In 1959, the position of the South Vietnam government had become desperate. President Eisenhower began sending large numbers of military advisers into Vietnam. Such a system had worked in Greece and in other countries; Western advisers had trained the troops and helped them withstand the onslaughts of Communist-trained guerrillas. By the spring of 1961, there were 5,000 American military advisers in Vietnam training the South Vietnamese troops.

Thus, America was catapulted into "interference." The presence of these troops was used as an excuse by the Northerners to step up their activity and support for the Viet Cong in the South. Ho Chi Minh began demanding the withdrawal of U.S. troops in 1961.

In the spring of 1962, American officials were talking about Vietnam incessantly. "The South Vietnamese face a long war, not of months but of years" said one. Who said this? Not President Kennedy's Secretary of State, Dean Rusk, but his Secretary of Defense, Robert McNamara. Thus was foreign policy made in 1962.

By 1963, President Kennedy had increased the American military commitment to 17,000 troops. That year the situation in Vietnam became more unstable when Premier Ngo Dinh Diem and his brother Ngo Dinh Nhu were murdered in an uprising of the generals of the army. The next year, the fateful moment came.

That moment was occasioned by an attack on an American destroyer in the Gulf of Tonkin in August, 1964, by North Vietnamese torpedo boats. Thus spurred, the American Congress authorized President Johnson to take the necessary steps to maintain peace, and the United States went into an undeclared war in Vietnam. This joint resolution of Congress, which made it possible for the American President to commit hundreds of thousands of troops to fighting without a declaration of war, was called the Tonkin Gulf resolution. In the years since 1964, the resolution has been debated scores of times, and from the debates has come one fact: the resolution ranks with the Monroe Doctrine or any other single action by Congress as one of the basic instruments of American foreign policy. Before the Tonkin Gulf resolution, no American President could commit large American forces to military action. There had been a succession of American interferences in the affairs of foreign nations, particularly in Latin America and in Haiti, over the years. In the Eisenhower years, American troops had gone into Lebanon to help stabilize that country (1958). But the Tonkin Gulf resolution allowed an American President to make war, for the first time in history, without consulting the Congress and securing a declaration of war. Its supporters suggested that affairs move too quickly in this modern world to have it otherwise. Opponents declared that the resolution must be outlawed to preserve liberty at home.

In 1965, the war in Vietnam became an American war. A year later, there were 190,000 troops in Vietnam in January and 390,000 in November. By 1967, even General William Westmoreland was saying that he could not see any end to the war in sight. The State Department, under Secretary Rusk, was trying to make a peace in which South Vietnam would be guaranteed its independence, but the fact was that Hanoi could see how the war was draining the United States and proposed to continue it, seeking settlement on its own terms. The war, the first major entanglement of the United States on the Asiatic continent, dragged on. The number of troops rose to over half a million.

In 1968 the Congress that had so unwisely given up its power to control wars decided to re-enter the picture. Senator William Fulbright of Arkansas, the chairman of the Senate Foreign Relations Committee, conducted an acerbic series of hearings at which the star witness was Secretary Rusk. The Secretary of State indicated that the administration had no intention of restoring to Congress its old role in policy decision.

How important Vietnam had become was shown in 1968. President Johnson was so unpopular that he decided against running for re-election. He undertook to de-escalate the war in Vietnam, but he achieved only limited success in restoring his own popularity or in cutting down the war. He initiated peace talks with the Vietminh in Paris.

But two years later, nothing had happened in the peace talks. The men of Hanoi were not to be moved. The Nixon administration, seeking disengagement from the war, decided to follow a policy of planned withdrawal of troops, and by the summer of 1969 had withdrawn 75,000 American soldiers from the Asiatic mainland. In September, President Nixon said he hoped to have all American troops out of the old Indochina territory by the fall of 1970.

Yet in 1970, the trouble seemed to be worsening. The war spread to Laos and Cambodia, and American advisers were present there, too. Hanoi's policy was obviously to prevent the disengagement of the United States from the war, to embarrass the United States as much as possible.

And through all this miasma of the 1960's and early 1970's certain facts had become very clear, although they were not very clearly stated by anyone in power. The emergence and endurance of Fidel Castro's revolutionary Cuba in the face of American opposition, the reaction of American students— who began in the 1960's to go to Cuba and help the Cubans cut their sugar, in defiance of American laws against travel to that island—gave an indication of a new force moving in on the making of American policy. The force was a public opinion force, expressed in a new way, not a nice way, not an orderly way, but a way long familiar in Europe and older countries, where students had for many decades been harbingers of change. Young Americans, making decisions of their own, defected to Canada, risking the loss of American citizenship, rather than join the military forces; or they went to Cuba, willing to face the disapproval and even prosecution of their government when they came home.

The students seemed to be saying something, if anyone was listening. And many people were listening to this voice of youth, which advised the policy makers that young America was not willing to live in a world dominated by power politics. Whether the young could devise, or force their elders to devise, some more reasonable solution to world affairs than that which had been imposed to this time was debatable. But

William P. Rogers

never before had power politics, the naked exercise of power which all strong countries had used in one way or another (for example, extension of the war in Vietnam until peace can be achieved on United States terms) been challenged so strongly in America. Here was hope. Even as the office of Secretary of State declined in importance in the management of foreign policy, pressures were brought to make the President of the United States, and all whom he employed, more responsive to a public opinion that made itself heard in riots and demonstrations. Publicly, for the first time, the activities of such secret organizations as the Central Intelligence Agency were questioned, and the suspicion was grave that the CIA was in Southeast Asia at least fomenting policy action as it had done in Cuba in the days of the unsuccessful Bay of Pigs invasion that dimmed the prestige of the new Kennedy administration.

It would be foolhardy to say that the Department of State has lost forever its primary position in the determination of foreign policy with the President. However, it is obvious that in the Eisenhower, Kennedy, and Johnson administrations the erosion had been severe; and the Nixon administration's Secretary of Defense Laird seemed to occupy the stage more than Secretary of State William P. Rogers. Such apparent declines had occurred before, in Wilson's time and in others; in ten years' time the swing might be the other way.

Whatever is to occur in the future, certain facts had become clear in the 1960's and early 1970's: the pressure was very definitely on the Americans and the Russians to cease using power as the most powerful nations had used it before them. And in America, the pressure was from within, stronger than it had ever been before.

Selected Bibliography

Acheson, Dean, *Present at the Creation: My Years in the State Department,* Norton, 1969.

Adams, Henry, *History of the United States,* 9 Vols., Hillary House Publishers, 1889.

Memoirs of John Quincy Adams, Comprising Portions of His Diary from 1795 to 1848, 12 Vols., Books for Libraries, Inc.

Beard, Charles A. and Mary R., *Beard's New Basic History of the United States,* edited by William Beard, rev. ed., Doubleday, 1960.

Franklin, Benjamin, *Autobiography.*

Hoyt, Edwin P., *John Quincy Adams,* Reilly and Lee Co., 1963.

Hunt, Gaillard, *The Department of State of the U.S., Its History and Functions.*

The writings of Thomas Jefferson.

Morison, Samuel Eliot, *Oxford History of the American People,* Oxford University Press, 1965.

Stuart, Graham H., *The Department of State.*

Van Doren, Carl, *Benjamin Franklin,* Viking Press, 1956.

Index

Organization of American States, 227

Oxford History of the American People, 75

Page, Walter Hines, 170
Paine, Thomas, 25, 27
Pakenham, Minister, 100-102
Panama Canal, 108, 128, 135, 156
Panama Conference, 79-81
Pan-American Conference, 191
Pan-American Union, 144
Parrott, W.S., 104
Patent Office, 77
Pax Germanica, 176
Pearl Harbor, 209
Penn family, 9, 12-13
Penn, William, 9, 20
Personal diplomacy, 215
Pétain, Marshal, 208
Philippines, 154
Pickering, Timothy, 45, 47, 49-50, 52
Pierce, Franklin, 110
Pinckney, Charles, 47
Pitt, William, 15
Polk, James K., 98, 100-101, 103-105, 108, 112
Portugal, American relations with, 26
Potsdam, 217
Pratt, Charles, 12
Present at the Creation, 237
Princeton, USS, 96
Protocol, 26, 120-121
Public Advertiser, 16

Public opinion force, 240, 242
Puerto Rico, 154

Quebec, 13, 23
Quebec Act, 23

Randolph, Edmund, 45
Randolph, John, 76-77
Recognition by the U.S. for foreign governments, 42-43, 108, 110, 165, 174, 198-199, 233
Remson, Henry, Jr., 41
Reparations plan, 190
Republic of La Plata, 65-66
Revolutionary War, 19
Rinaldo, 124
Rogers, William P., 242
Roosevelt, Franklin Delano, 200-202, 204, 206-209, 211, 213-215, 220, 233
Roosevelt, Theodore, 152, 156, 158, 161, 175
Root, Elihu, 156, 158, 161, 184
Rusk, Dean, 44, 231, 238-239
Russia (Soviet Union), American relations with, 28, 67, 127, 182, 189, 199, 204-205, 215, 217-218, 220-221, 231
Rutledge, Edward, 24

Sackville-West affair, 141-142
Sackville-West, Lionel, 141-142

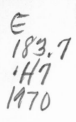